PRAYERSCRIPTS

GIVE US THE NATIONS

Prayers That Release God's Rule Over Every Nation

CYRIL OPOKU

VOLUME ONE
Afghanistan–Myanmar

Give Us the Nations: Prayers That Release God's Rule Over Every Nation (Volume One: Books 1 to 4)
© 2025 Cyril Opoku. PrayerScripts. All rights reserved.

No part of this publication may be reproduced, stored in a retrieval system, or transmitted in any form or by any means—electronic, mechanical, photocopy, recording, or otherwise—without the prior written permission of the publisher, except in the case of brief quotations used in reviews, articles, or devotionals.

Published by *Quest Publications (questpublications@outlook.com)*
ISBN: 978-1-988439-97-6

Unless otherwise indicated, all Scripture quotations are taken from the World English Bible WEB, which is in the public domain. For more information, visit: www.worldenglish.bible

© Operation World Source Acknowledgment

> The country information, key statistics, prayer points, maps, and national flags featured in this book have been used with grateful acknowledgment from Operation World, published by InterVarsity Press (IVP).
>
> **Source:** *Operation World: The Definitive Prayer Guide to Every Nation,* 7th Edition, edited by Jason Mandryk. © Operation World Resources / WEC International. Used by permission.
>
> Operation World is a ministry of WEC International and remains a vital global resource mobilizing prayer for the nations. For more information, visit www.operationworld.org.
>
> All rights to Operation World materials remain with their respective copyright holders.
>
> The prayers in this book are original works inspired by, but not reproduced from, Operation World content.

This book is a work of devotional encouragement. It is not intended to replace biblical study, pastoral counsel, or professional therapy.

Printed in the United States of America.
First Edition: October 2025
For more books like this, visit *PrayerScripts:* https://prayerscripts.org

Contents

Contents .... *iii*
Preface .... *viii*
Introduction .... *x*
How to Use PrayerScripts .... *xii*

1. Afghanistan 1
2. Albania 4
3. Algeria 6
4. American Samoa 8
5. Andorra 10
6. Angola 12
7. Anguilla 15
8. Antigua and Barbuda 17
9. Argentina 19
10. Armenia 21
11. Aruba 23
12. Australia 25
13. Austria 27
14. Azerbaijan 29
15. The Bahamas 31
16. Bahrain 33
17. Bangladesh 35
18. Barbados 37
19. Belarus 39
20. Belgium 41
21. Belize 43
22. Benin 46
23. Bermuda 48
24. Bhutan 50
25. Bolivia 52

26. Bosnia and Herzegovina 54
27. Botswana 56
28. Brazil 58
29. British Virgin Islands 60
30. Brunei 62
31. Bulgaria 64
32. Burkina Faso 66
33. Burundi 68
34. Cabo Verde 70
35. Cambodia 72
36. Cameroon 74
37. Canada 76
38. Cayman Islands 78
39. Central African Republic 80
40. Chad 82
41. Chile 84
42. People's Republic of China 86
43. Colombia 88
44. Comoros 90
45. Republic of Congo (ROC) 92
46. Democratic Republic of Congo (DRC) 94
47. Cook Islands 96
48. Costa Rica 98
49. Côte d'Ivoire 100
50. Croatia 102
51. Cuba 104
52. Curaçao 106
53. Cyprus 108
54. Czechia 110
55. Denmark 112
56. Djibouti 114
57. Dominica 116

58. Dominican Republic 118
59. Ecuador 120
60. Egypt 122
61. El Salvador 124
62. Equatorial Guinea 126
63. Eritrea 128
64. Estonia 130
65. Eswatini 132
66. Ethiopia 134
67. Falkland Islands 136
68. Faroe Islands 138
69. Federated States of Micronesia 140
70. Fiji 142
71. Finland 144
72. France 146
73. French Guiana 148
74. French Polynesia 150
75. Gabon 152
76. The Gambia 154
77. Georgia 156
78. Germany 158
79. Ghana 160
80. Gibraltar 162
81. Greece 164
82. Greenland 166
83. Grenada 168
84. Guadeloupe 170
85. Guam 172
86. Guatemala 174
87. Guinea 176
88. Guinea-Bissau 178
89. Guyana 180

90. Haiti 182
91. Holy See (Vatican City) 184
92. Honduras 186
93. Hong Kong 188
94. Hungary 190
95. Iceland 192
96. India 194
97. Indonesia 196
98. Iran 198
99. Iraq 200
100. Ireland 202
101. Israel 204
102. Italy 206
103. Jamaica 208
104. Japan 211
105. Jordan 213
106. Kazakhstan 215
107. Kenya 217
108. Kiribati 219
109. Kosovo 221
110. Kuwait 223
111. Kyrgyzstan 225
112. Laos 227
113. Latvia 229
114. Lebanon 231
115. Lesotho 233
116. Liberia 235
117. Libya 237
118. Liechtenstein 239
119. Lithuania 241
120. Luxembourg 243
121. Macau 245

122. Madagascar ... 247
123. Malawi ... 249
124. Malaysia ... 251
125. Maldives ... 253
126. Mali ... 255
127. Malta ... 257
128. Marshall Islands ... 259
129. Martinique ... 261
130. Mauritania ... 263
131. Mauritius ... 265
132. Mayotte ... 267
133. Mexico ... 269
134. Moldova ... 271
135. Monaco ... 273
136. Mongolia ... 275
137. Montenegro ... 277
138. Montserrat ... 279
139. Morocco ... 281
140. Mozambique ... 283
141. Myanmar ... 285

Epilogue ... 287
Encourage Others with Your Story ... 289
More from PrayerScripts ... 290

Preface

"Ask of me, and I will give you the nations for your inheritance, the uttermost parts of the earth for your possession."
— Psalm 2:8 WEB

The Father's invitation in Psalm 2:8 is the hinge of history: Heaven calls, and the Church is summoned to respond. This single verse compresses a cosmic economy—an inheritance given to the Son and a mandate extended to His people to ask, to intercede, and to receive. It tells us two indispensable truths: first, that the nations belong to God and are intended to be His possession; second, that the Kingdom advances through the prayers and petitions of those who will partner with God's heart. This book is born from that summons. It is not a casual collection of sentiments; it is a strategic, scripture-saturated tool for believers who will stand in the gap and press Heaven's claims into earthly places.

As you open this book you are entering into intercessory territory. Each page is designed to connect your voice to the Father's will. The prayers are not abstract theology; they are operational declarations—worded to align with the Scriptures and aimed to break principalities, to heal social and spiritual wounds, and to establish Christ's rule where darkness now holds sway. You will find that the tone throughout is both reverent and militant: reverent toward God's holiness and militant against anything that resists His reign. This is the language of prophetic prayer—strong, tender, and obedient to the Word.

This first volume in the series gathers **141 nations—from Afghanistan through Myanmar**—each with its unique landscape of need and opportunity. The content you will pray through is informed by careful research and guided by the Holy Spirit's promptings. These prayers are meant to be prayed aloud, to be stood upon, and to be repeated in faith. They are for intercessors, pastors, house-church leaders, and ordinary believers who refuse to leave the nations to chance. As you pray, expect the Holy Spirit to refine your heart, enlarge your vision, and deepen your resolve to see God's Kingdom established among the peoples named here.

Pray boldly. Ask big. This is your inheritance—ask of the Lord, and He will give us the nations.

Till He Comes!
Cyril O. *(Virginia, October 2025)*

Introduction

The world will not be won by mere programs, policies, or polite conversation. The nations will be possessed by fervent, disciplined, and sustained prayer.

If you are tired of shallow, incidental praying for global issues, prepare to be provoked. This book demands more than sentiment; it challenges you to become a persistent presence in the affairs of the nations. The Church's destiny is global, and our stewardship of that destiny is exercised through prayer that is strategic, scriptural, and sustained.

What you hold in your hands is a manual for spiritual government. Each country section begins with a selected Scripture from the World English Bible, chosen to anchor the prayer in God's revealed truth. The Scripture is followed by a Spirit-led, first-person prophetic intercession crafted to release God's rule into that nation's life. These prayers are written to be spoken aloud and to be used in corporate settings as well as private devotion. They are intentionally structured to match both the spiritual realities and the practical statistics that shape each nation's context: demographics, religious landscape, social challenges, and existing openings for the Gospel. This is not guesswork; it is informed intercession.

Operation World has been acknowledged for its meticulous research and global perspective, and its data informed the focus that shaped each prayer. That partnership between careful human research and heavenly revelation is vital. We bring facts to our knees and marry them with faith. The result is not a report but an activation—words that carry authority because they are saturated with Scripture and shaped by situational reality. Expect prayers that confront principalities, plead for justice, heal ethnic wounds, protect children, strengthen churches, and prepare leaders—spiritual and civic—for righteousness.

How have these prayers been written? With four guiding commitments: (1) Scriptural fidelity—each petition is rooted in God's Word; (2) Contextual sensitivity—each prayer interacts with the realities faced by the nation's people; (3) Prophetic boldness—the language is declarative and expectant; and (4) Pastoral tenderness—while prophetic, the tone is pastoral, caring for people in their pain. You will see prayers that name systems (corruption, trafficking, animism), that call heaven's justice to earth, and that plant Kingdom solutions (leaders of integrity, discipleship movements, social restoration). These are not theoretical; they are task-oriented and prayer-operational.

This book is designed to convert readers into intercessors and intercessors into governors in prayer. It will stretch you. It will grieve you. It will fuel you. Pray these prayers faithfully, join other believers in petition, and allow this work to form a habit of national intercession. The nations wait. The King has asked. Will you answer?

How to Use PrayerScripts

This book is designed as a daily companion to guide you into a prophetic lifestyle of prayer. This is a prayer journey meant to position you to walk in the fullness of God's promises. Here's how to make the most of it:

1. Dedicate a Daily Time:

Set aside a consistent time each day to engage with the prayer for that day. Treat this as sacred time with God, where distractions are minimized, and your heart is fully focused on communion with Him. Ten to twenty minutes daily is sufficient to meditate on the Scripture, pray, and receive revelation.

2. Begin with Scripture Reflection:

Each day begins with a carefully selected Scripture. Read it slowly, meditate on its meaning, and let the Holy Spirit illuminate how it applies to your life. Allow the Word to penetrate your spirit and prepare you to pray from a place of faith and expectancy.

3. Pray the Guided Prayer:

Use the prayer provided as a framework, allowing it to resonate with your own words and personal circumstances. Speak each declaration with authority and confidence, fully believing that God is at work. You may also pause to personalize the prayer for your specific family, career, or ministry needs.

- **Make It Personal**

  These prayers are written in the first person so you can make them your own. Speak them aloud, inserting the names of your family members, your workplace, your church, or your city where applicable. The more you personalize the prayer, the more you will sense its power shaping your reality.

- **Pray with Authority**

  These are not timid requests; they are bold decrees. Lift your voice as a covenant child of God, covered by the blood of Jesus and backed by heaven's authority. When you pray, do so with confidence that Christ has already won the victory on your behalf.

- **Leave Room for the Holy Spirit**

  These written prayers are a guide, not a limit. As you pray, pause to listen. The Holy Spirit may give you prophetic words, insights, or specific instructions. Follow His lead. Allow Him to expand the prayer, add declarations, or guide you into deeper intercession.

4. Journal Your Insights:

Keep a notebook or journal to record any thoughts, revelations, or confirmations you receive during prayer. Writing down what God speaks to you helps solidify understanding and creates a record of breakthrough and growth over time.

5. Repeat as Needed:

Some prayers or themes may need to be revisited multiple times. Answer to prayer is progressive; the more you engage with these prayers in faith, the greater the manifestation in your life and household. You can return to this book at any season to reinforce your victory and dominion.

6. Live in Expectancy:

Prayer is only one part of walking in enlargement—your actions, faith, and obedience amplify the power of these prayers. Move boldly into opportunities, embrace the doors God opens, and live with a confident expectation that God is answering your prayer beyond what you can see or imagine.

By following this guide daily, you will cultivate a lifestyle of prayer and kingdom impact. Let this book be your companion as you step into the new dimensions God has destined for you.

1

AFGHANISTAN

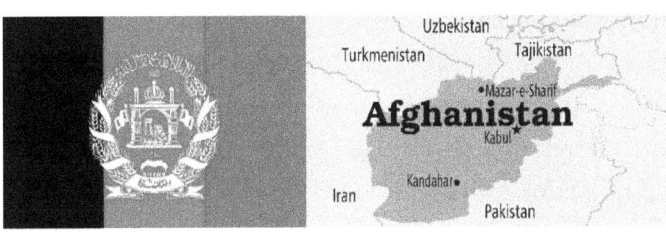

Yahweh will also be a high tower for the oppressed; a high tower in times of trouble.
— Psalm 9:9-10 WEB

Almighty and compassionate King, I come as a burning intercessor and I declare Your shelter over Afghanistan. Sovereign Lord of heaven and earth, who judges with righteousness and lifts up the lowly, I call Your refuge to stand like a strong, unassailable tower over Kabul and every village from the valleys to the mountains. I proclaim that the oppressed shall find safety in Your presence, that those crushed by fear, hunger, and violent rule will discover a fortress none can penetrate except by Your will. I speak Your protection over the few who confess Christ there and over the secret gospel workers who risk everything; preserve their lives and make them living witnesses even under danger.

Father, by the full power of Your Word I plead for mercy where persecution is most fierce. Where the rule of men has reintroduced harsh laws, where women are silenced and barred from public life, send Your justice like a river and Your deliverance like a flood. For those who are hunted because they believe, break every chain and confuse every scheme set against them. For the impoverished and those left destitute after earthquakes and economic collapse, be their Provider—supply food, healing, shelter, and the medical care mothers and newborns so desperately need. Let the truth of Christ's worth and love be communicated through clandestine radios, secret Scriptures, and sacrificial neighbors; let those mediums multiply and bear fruit.

Lord Jesus, You who gave the nations to Your people in inheritance, release strategies of salvation over every ethno-linguistic people in Afghanistan—Pashtu and Dari, Turkmen, Uzbek and others. Raise up courageous Afghan disciples and shepherds who will shepherd hidden flocks and lead with humility. Soften hearts in the leadership and insert dreams and visions of the Savior into the hearts of the lost. Turn cycles of violence into seasons of repentance and revival; let hunger bring people to their knees before the Bread of Life. Empower international and local aid to reach those barred by politics, and flood the land with the gospel through creative channels.

Holy Spirit, fall on Afghan women with revelation of their identity in Christ; bring rescue, dignity, health and courage. Break the spiritual system that binds them; appoint guardians of mercy, extend legal favor, and cause birthing places to be safe with midwives and doctors where needed. I command fear to loose its grip: let testimony and prayer multiply, persecution be exposed and converted into opportunity for gospel advance. I decree that

Afghanistan will not be forgotten by heaven—that the prayer of many will usher in a harvest of souls and the rule of the Kingdom will expand until every mountain and valley declares Your reign. In Jesus' name, Amen.

2

ALBANIA

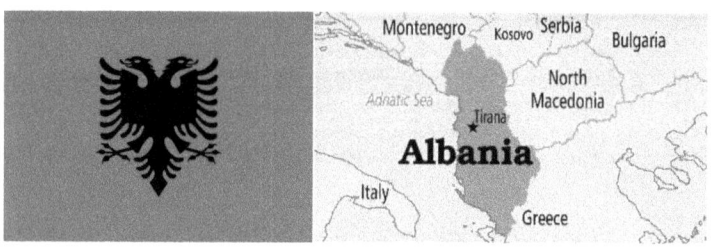

> May God be merciful to us, bless us, and cause his face to shine upon us; that your way may be known on earth, and your salvation among all nations.
> — Psalm 67:1-2 WEB

Magnificent and merciful King, arise and let Your favor rest upon Albania. I stand in the gap as a watchman and prophet, declaring that the mercy of God will continue to move upon Tirana and every town and village. I praise You for the growth already seen and I speak blessing now—that Your face would shine with favor over the Albanian Church, over the Albanian Evangelical Alliance, and over every indigenous leader who carries a shepherd's heart. May the blessing that raised up small beginnings into nationwide networks deepen; may grace multiply pastors, disciples, and sending bodies that will reach beyond Albania's borders.

Gracious Father, as Your ways are made known through renewed evangelism and discipleship, I pray for consolidation of spiritual fruit: strengthen leadership training, protect networks from division, and give wisdom for sustainable discipleship. Where instability tempts compromise, give clarity and courage to stand on Your unchanging truth. Bless the literate and hospitable hearts of this people; convert their high literacy and cultural strengths into vehicles for Scripture engagement, Bible distribution, and discipleship movements. Raise up gospel media, Bible study material in Albanian, and a fresh wave of prophetic worship that will make Your salvation known among the nations.

Lord of harvest, I ask that Albania's churches will increasingly send—not merely receive—workers to the unreached. Multiply a missionary mindset; empower Youth With A Mission and local sending agencies to plant churches in diaspora communities and unreached regions. Root out any complacency born of religious tradition and ignite a holy hunger for lost souls. Protect the small evangelical minority from spiritual weariness; anoint their families, marriages, and ministries with provision and apostolic favor.

Holy Spirit, continue to fan the prayers that opened Albania; let prayer movements be rekindled and link the churches to the global body for greater impact. I declare that Albania will shine as a conduit of God's mercy and blessing to surrounding lands; that the way of the Lord will be known on earth through Albanian witness, and that salvation will flow as a river from this nation to many nations. In Jesus' name, Amen.

3

ALGERIA

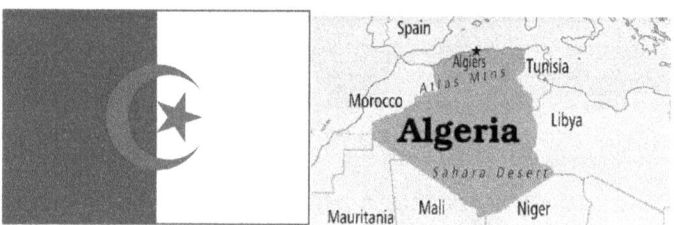

Arise, shine; for your light has come, and Yahweh's glory has risen on you!
— Isaiah 60:1 WEB

Lord of light and glory, I come with prophetic intensity, declaring that Your glory has risen over Algeria and the darkness that once held its millions will be pierced by supernatural light. I lift up the Berber and Arab peoples before Your throne, and I decree liberation: where hearts were hardened by religion or fear, breathe new life; where prejudice divided communities, pour unity. I celebrate the growth of the Algerian Church as evidence of Your hand, and I ask for an increase—more workers, more Bibles, more accessible Christian resources in Arabic, Tamazight, and French so that the persecuted can hear, read, and teach. Let literature, radio, and portable media be multiplied and protected by Your guardian angels.

Mighty Redeemer, protect the believers who have come through visions and personal evangelism; surround their fellowships with hidden strength. Where pressure rises and governments restrict, clothe leaders with wisdom and grant supernatural boldness tempered by discretion. Strengthen the unity that marks Algerian congregations; let ethnic history be healed by the cross so that the Church's witness across Kabyle and Arab communities shines as the body of Christ. Send encouragers, trainers and apostolic teams to bolster local leadership and expand correspondence courses and satellite ministry that can reach unreached millions.

Jehovah Jireh, provide for the persecuted: deliver those arrested, defend those threatened, and release legal favor where possible. Prosper the distribution of Scriptures and discipleship materials, and give creativity for covert evangelism that honors You while protecting lives. Raise up a new generation of young Algerian disciples who will use media, music, and testimony to make the gospel culturally resonant and impossible to ignore. Let healing, freedom and repentance sweep cities from Algiers to remote villages.

Holy Spirit, we declare an unstoppable advance of Your Kingdom in Algeria: darkness retreats, strongholds fall, and the rule of Christ is established in hearts, homes, and families. I prophesy that the Church's growth will accelerate and that Algeria will be a strategic outpost of witness in North Africa, a light to neighboring nations. Empower the persecuted to be joyful witnesses and turn pressure into momentum for mass conversions. In Jesus' name, Amen.

4

AMERICAN SAMOA

> Go and make disciples of all nations, baptizing them in the name of the Father and of the Son and of the Holy Spirit;
> — Matthew 28:19 WEB

Sovereign Lord and Master of the harvest, I come with thanksgiving for the spiritual fruit in American Samoa and I declare Your Great Commission power to rest on these islands. Majesty and mercy, bless Pago Pago and every village as a sending base; let the devotion of the Assemblies of God, YWAM, and local churches be multiplied into a powerful missionary impulse. I speak apostolic favor on training centers, on youth ministries, and on those discipling the Samoan people—that this land, richly Christian, will not keep the blessing inward but will spill it outward to the nations.

Gracious Savior, use the high literacy and vibrant church networks to deepen discipleship and raise up leaders who are missional by calling. Strengthen theological formation, protect families, and give provision for long-term mission initiatives. I ask that islands be launched as hubs for Pacific outreach: equip Samoan missionaries with language skills, cultural insight, and supernatural favor in neighboring islands and beyond. Bless the works of YWAM and other mobilizers; multiply short-term teams into long-term partnerships that plant churches and make disciples.

Lord, keep the flame of revival alive in a culture that can drift into complacency. Where material comfort or cultural drift threatens, awaken a hunger for holiness, a renewed commitment to prayer, and a fresh love for the lost. Empower worship to break spiritual inertia and shape a generation that values sacrificial giving, persistent prayer, and courageous evangelism. Let every school, clinic, harbor, and marketplace be a place where the gospel is proclaimed and lives are transformed.

Holy Spirit, I decree that American Samoa will be known not just for its faithfulness but as a sending nation—islands of light releasing workers, Scripture, and compassion across the Pacific and the world. May Christ's name be glorified in every home, and may the Kingdom's rule be evident in government, education, and family life. In Jesus' name, Amen.

5

ANDORRA

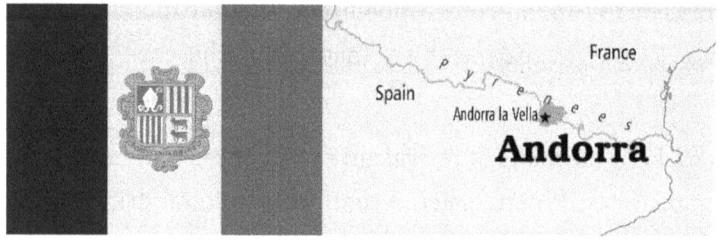

> For the love of money is a root of all kinds of evil. Some have been led astray from the faith in their greed, and have pierced themselves through with many sorrows.
> — 1 Timothy 6:10 WEB

Righteous Judge and gentle Savior, I stand in prayer over Andorra la Vella and I declare the truth that conquers the lie of materialism: riches are not the source of lasting joy, only Christ is. I prophetically call heaven's reproof into the places where duty-free wealth, finance and tourism have seduced hearts. Let the allure of goods be exposed as empty and let conscience be awakened; may the people of Andorra discover the surpassing worth of knowing Christ more than any earthly treasure. I speak repentance into boardrooms, marketplaces, and family estates so greed is dethroned and generosity is enthroned.

Lord of all, pour out a holy discontent with materialism that drives Andorrans to seek You. Raise up a faithful handful of churches and evangelicals who will shine in simplicity, sacrificial service, and gospel witness. Use that small evangelical presence to create disproportionate spiritual influence: workplace witness, mercy ministries for the marginalized, and creative outreach to tourists and financiers. Transform the culture of consumption into a culture of hospitality, stewardship, and worship.

Almighty Redeemer, bless the literate and cosmopolitan communities with Gospel humility. Give pastors courage to preach Jesus over prosperity messages and wisdom to address financial temptations with biblical truth. Establish ministries that meet real needs—addiction support, counseling for those pierced by the pursuit of wealth, and places of refuge for the lonely—so the Church's witness is compassionate and credible.

Holy Spirit, I decree that Andorra will be released from the tyranny of materialism; that former smugglers' shadows will be replaced by the light of Christ. Let the few believers become salt and light in a culture of abundance so that many will consider the eternal over the ephemeral. Raise up a new movement of simple, generous disciples who will see Thy Kingdom come and Thy will be done in this principality. In Jesus' name, Amen.

6

Angola

> The Lord Yahweh's Spirit is on me, because Yahweh has anointed me to preach good news to the humble. He has sent me to bind up the broken hearted, to proclaim liberty to the captives and release to those who are bound.
> —Isaiah 61:1 WEB.

Almighty and Sovereign Father, King over the nations, I come as a mighty intercessor and declare Your anointing on Angola now. I stand in the breach for Luanda and for every village from Cunene to Cabinda and I cry that the Spirit who brings good news would saturate every heart and every home. I lift before Your throne the millions who live under the weight of trauma from decades of war, the children and the 47% who are under fifteen, and I command the binding of brokenness and the release of hope—because You have sent One to bind up the brokenhearted and to proclaim liberty to the captives. I declare

Your healing over the memory and wounds of that long conflict; where pain has rooted itself, let Your Spirit loosen it and plant resurrection life.

Lord Jesus, I pray for the Church in Angola: strengthen your remnant, raise up shepherds trained in Your Word, and root out falsehoods, fear, and witchcraft with the clear light of the gospel. Let evangelical fervor that grew in the darkest years now mature into discipleship that multiplies trained pastors, biblical literacy, and holy living. Convert the strongholds of animism and fear by demonstrations of Your love—feed the poor through Your hands, house the homeless through Your people, and comfort the traumatised through Your presence. Where Islam's message is spreading through money and simplicity, give your Church wisdom and compassion to meet needs and present the fullness of Christ.

Gracious Father, I intercede for justice and economic shalom: close the gap that scars Luanda with extreme wealth and the rural heart with dire poverty; turn oil wealth from self-enrichment into provision and infrastructure that blesses the poor. Pour out Your spirit of reconciliation: teach forgiveness, break cycles of vengeance, and make the Church an instrument of social healing. Raise prophetic and godly leaders who will steward resources, prioritize the vulnerable, and govern with integrity. By Your Spirit, let the Church be a refuge for trauma recovery—counseling, restoration ministries, and communities that model love in action.

I declare, by faith, that Angola will know the reign of Jesus: Thy Kingdom come, Thy will be done across the provinces, in markets, in homes, and in halls of power. Let righteousness spring up; let praise be heard from rural fields to the capital's streets. Send revival that brings repentance, trained shepherds, and a multiplying people who live holy and love boldly. May every unevangelized place see light, and may the blood of Christ cover and make Angola untouchable for the enemy. In Jesus' name, Amen.

7

ANGUILLA

> If my people who are called by my name will humble themselves, pray, seek my face, and turn from their wicked ways, then I will hear from heaven, will forgive their sin, and will heal their land.
> —2 Chronicles 7:14 WEB.

Sovereign Lord of heaven and earth, I come before You on behalf of tiny Anguilla and declare Your healing and revival over this island remnant. I stand as an intercessor and call Your attention to this community—its streets, its churches, its people—asking that Your eyes be open and Your ears attentive. I plead for humility, prayer, and turning among those who call upon Your name; I ask that when Your people bow in true repentance and seek Your face, You will hear from heaven, forgive, and bring fresh healing and awakening to every heart and habit.

Lord, breathe new spiritual life into religious tradition so that the form becomes fire and the ritual becomes revival. Let churches that may rest on ancestral faith be stirred into zeal, authenticity, and kingdom action. Raise up young leaders, worshipers, and evangelists who will not allow this island to be bypassed by the Spirit. Where complacency or cultural Christianity has dulled hunger, fan holy hunger and devotion—that families, schools, and marketplaces might be transformed by the presence of Christ and the power of Scripture lived out in love.

Father, pour out mercy upon Anguilla's civic leaders and influencers: give them wisdom to govern with compassion, integrity, and a desire to see the vulnerable flourish. Let literacy and prosperity be channels for blessing, not pride; protect the island from spiritual deception and from any subtle drift toward empty tradition. Empower the churches to serve in practical ways—outreach to the elderly, mentoring youth, and being the hands that meet needs—so that the gospel is seen as healing action.

By faith I declare a new season: Your presence will not be a distant memory but a living reality in Anguilla. Turn this remnant into a lighthouse for the Caribbean—small in size but great in joy, radical in love, and powerful in prayer. Let revival come that births holiness, unity, and outward mission until Thy Kingdom comes and Thy will is done on this island as in heaven. In Jesus' name, Amen.

8

ANTIGUA AND BARBUDA

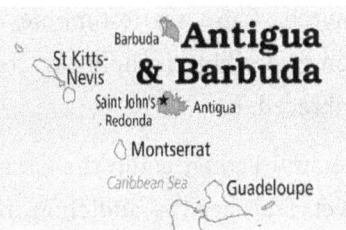

> Yahweh, you have been favorable to your land. You have restored the fortunes of Jacob. ... Won't you revive us again, that your people may rejoice in you?
> —Psalm 85:1,6 WEB.

Almighty God, Governor of heaven's host, I come before Your throne and cry aloud for Antigua and Barbuda—for St. John's and for every parish and isle. I declare Your favor over this land and ask that You restore what has grown weary, rekindle what has grown cold, and revive what is routine. I speak to complacency in churches and culture, and I command a holy shaking that awakens hearts to earnest prayer, sacrificial service, and courageous witness. Let Your people no longer be satisfied with mere tradition; stir deep repentance and a hunger for Your glory.

Lord Jesus, pour out a fresh wind of revival that unites congregations and mobilizes believers to impact society with compassion and truth. Empower pastors, youth leaders, teachers, and families to be lights in education, government, and commerce. Replace complacency with courageous love that confronts moral decay and social injustice—that anti-life choices, corruption, and apathy would be met by an organized, prayerful, and loving Church. Raise up testimonies of transformed lives: men and women walking in holiness, communities healed, and the poor embraced.

Merciful Father, equip the Church with practical ministries that meet real needs—addiction recovery, family restoration, job training, and outreach to the marginalized. Let the literacy and life expectancy advantages be used to multiply kingdom influence, not comfort. Give students, seminaries, and small groups a fresh vision for evangelism so that this overwhelmingly Christian nation becomes overwhelmingly Christlike, bearing witness across cultural and class lines.

I declare, by faith, that Antigua and Barbuda will be a people who rejoice in You; revival will produce joy, obedience, and public righteousness. Let the cry rise: Thy Kingdom come; may government, education, and family submit to Christ's rule. May this nation send out workers of grace, not just maintain pleasant religion, and may the name of Jesus be honored in every street and shore. In Jesus' name, Amen.

9

ARGENTINA

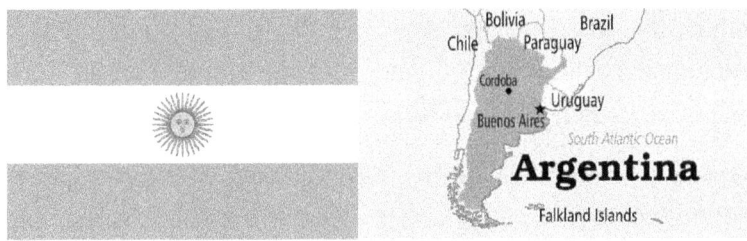

> But you will receive power when the Holy Spirit has come upon you. You will be witnesses to me in Jerusalem, in all Judea and Samaria, and to the uttermost parts of the earth.
> —Acts 1:8 WEB.

Almighty King and Lord of all nations, I come before You for Argentina—Buenos Aires, the provinces, the slums, and the campuses. I declare Your empowering Spirit upon Argentine churches and believers: impart the boldness, wisdom, and supernatural power to be witnesses in the heart of the city, in the neighborhoods of the wealthy, and in the forgotten villas. I pray that the Holy Spirit would break cultural hardness in the educated and influential—that the cultured upper class, the Jewish community, and migrant groups would see Christ's life evidenced in gospel humility and love, not merely arguments.

Lord Jesus, awaken a missionary hunger among seminarians, Bible schools, and local pastors so that the surge in evangelical numbers matures into mature discipleship and outward mission. Turn every seminary and prayer meeting into a sending base; give ACIERA[1], councils of pastors, and leaders ears to hear what the Spirit is saying and the courage to act in unity. Bring revival to slums and street ministries; let the homeless, street kids, and slum dwellers encounter healing, food, dignity, and the gospel, and let those encounters ripple into transformed neighborhoods.

Gracious Father, break down ethnic and cultural walls: empower faithful witnesses among Jewish, Chinese, Korean, Japanese, and Vietnamese communities, and release resources for contextual ministry that honors heritage while proclaiming Christ. Raise up evangelists and teachers who combine doctrine and compassion, truth and service, so the gospel addresses both soul and society. Give government and civic leaders wisdom to steward Argentina's resources for the common good and protect the vulnerable from exploitation.

I declare, by faith, that Argentina will be a power for the Kingdom: the Spirit's power will turn institutions, families, and public life toward Jesus. May Buenos Aires be a sending city, not a place unreachable by the gospel; may unity and holy leadership arise; may the Church move in power to bless and to transform. Thy Kingdom come, Thy will be done across Argentina as it is in heaven. In Jesus' name, Amen.

---

[1] Local Councils of Pastors and the National Evangelical Alliance

10

Armenia

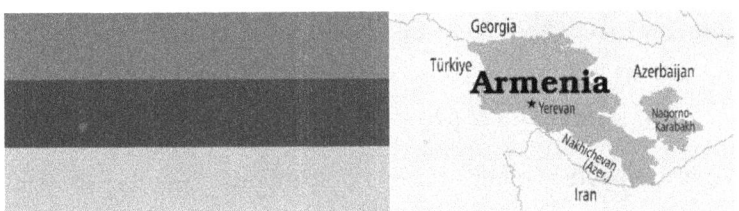

And he will judge between many peoples, and will decide concerning strong nations afar off. They will beat their swords into plowshares, and their spears into pruning hooks. Nation will not lift up sword against nation. Neither will they learn war any more.
—Micah 4:3 WEB.

Sovereign Lord of peace, ancient God who remembers the faithful, I come before You for Armenia—for Yerevan, for villages once more shaken, for the descendants of a people who first embraced You. I lift up the scars of genocide, the fear of renewed cleansing, and the sorrow of displacement. As an intercessor I plead: turn the hearts of the strong away from violence; let instruments of war be converted into tools of life. Where mistrust and bitterness have taken root, plant forgiveness; where fear has held families captive, release courageous trust in Your protection.

Lord Jesus, renew the Armenian Church with courage, wisdom, and reconciliation. Let the 1,700-year heritage not be a brittle memory but a living, missionary force—sending light across the region and into the diaspora. Give leaders and pastors prophetic boldness to teach forgiveness and practical peacemaking; let the Church become a reconciler, a healer of memories, and an offering of mercy to neighbours. As Russian support fades and geopolitical focus shifts, empower Armenians to look to You, not to princes, for security, identity, and hope.

Compassionate Father, raise up ministries of trauma care, reconciliation programs, and community development that transform fear into creativity and wounds into worship. Pour out Your Spirit on young people who will rebuild society with integrity and honor. Release a revival among the diaspora that fuels mission back to their homeland, and let Armenian believers be a light of mercy in the Middle East and beyond.

I declare, in faith, that Your rule will prevail: the sword will be beaten into plowshares across this region; peace will be more than a dream—it will be Your gift. May Armenia stand as a testimony that God's loving kindness endures and that His kingdom brings lasting justice and shalom. Thy Kingdom come, Thy will be done in this ancient land, now and forever. In Jesus' name, Amen.

11

ARUBA

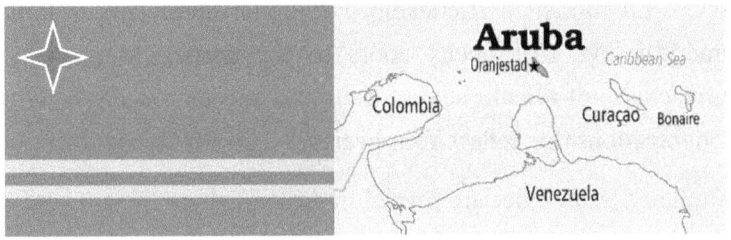

> You are witnesses of these things. Behold, I send out the promise of my Father on you. But wait in the city of Jerusalem until you are clothed with power from on high."
> — Luke 24:48-49 WEB

Sovereign Lord, King over the nations, I lift Aruba to You with a prophetic voice: let Your Spirit breathe fresh power and witness into this isle. I stand before Your throne and declare that the very promise of Spirit-empowered witness will fall upon every neighborhood, every Papiamento-speaking congregation, and every recent arrival from Latin America, the Caribbean, and Asia. As one who longs for Your kingdom to come, I ask that Your presence be manifest among the island's children and elders, in Oranjestad and every village, so that the high literacy and hearts poised to receive truth will not be wasted but welcomed into vibrant faith.

Father God, You know the mix of tongues and cultures—Dutch, Papiamento, English, Asian languages—and I ask You to weave them together into a holy tapestry of praise. Let churches that already speak English and Papiamento become hubs of Gospel hospitality to immigrants from Asia, bearing culturally wise witness in music, literature, and worship. Raise up messengers from among the immigrant communities; empower local believers to be intentional in friendship, vocational mentoring, and the practical love that opens doors to the gospel. May the 1% unreached not remain so, but be found and embraced by living congregations that reflect Your heart.

Almighty Jesus, I declare revival in Aruba: where the evangelical presence has grown unevenly, let multiplication occur. Break down any barriers of language, class, or custom that keep people apart. Let the island's strong Christian identity be deepened into Christ-centered discipleship, not merely cultural adherence. Raise leaders who are holy, credible, and humble; restore reputation where it has been wounded; clothe ministers with integrity so that the name of Christ is honored across all islands of influence.

Lord of the harvest, make Aruba a lighthouse in the Caribbean—a place where Your Kingdom advances through compassionate justice, transformed homes, and believers who steward education, tourism, and commerce for Your glory. I claim Acts 1:8 over this nation: send the power, send the witnesses, and let the remotest parts receive the gospel in truth and love. In Jesus' name, Amen.

12

Australia

The earth is the LORD's, and the fulness thereof; the world, and those who dwell in it.
— Psalm 24:1 WEB

Holy Creator and Owner of the land, I come as a bold intercessor for Australia, declaring Your sovereign claim over every mountain, plain, city, and coastline. I lift up Canberra, Sydney, Perth, and every town as territory belonging to the Lord of all. Where land and water have been overexploited, where stewardship has been treated as private privilege rather than sacred trust, I call heaven's attention: awaken repentance, humble leaders, and shape public policy toward sustainable, life-giving care. Let the knowledge that the earth and its fullness belong to You move the hearts of those who govern, farm, mine, and build.

Gracious Father, hear my prayer for the Church in Australia. Where influence has waned and credibility been wounded by scandal and secular shifts, revive a countercultural holiness that wins rather than offends. Raise up congregations that are winsome, transparent, and sacrificial; let them embody integrity in word and deed so public perception is transformed. Grant renewed passion for discipleship among younger generations and fresh, Spirit-led expressions of worship and mission that resonate across Australia's vast cultural diversity and among the twenty percent who use English as a second language.

Lord Jesus, for the fragile ecology and the recurring droughts and fires, release supernatural protection and wise stewardship. Equip scientists, farmers, and policymakers with wisdom, foresight, and cooperative resolve to steward water, restore landscapes, and develop clean energy that honors Your creation. Bring corporate repentance for exploitative consumption; turn industries toward regenerative practices. Let stewardship become a gospel outworking—where care for creation testifies to the Creator.

Mighty King, I prophesy revival that influences law, education, media, and family life. Let the Church rise as a redemptive force for social healing, addressing inequality, loneliness, and moral disorientation with gospel compassion. May Australian Christians pursue justice, mercy, and humility, recovering influence not by power but by love. I declare that the Lord's claim over this land will bring restoration, revival, and righteous governance. In Jesus' name, Amen.

13

AUSTRIA

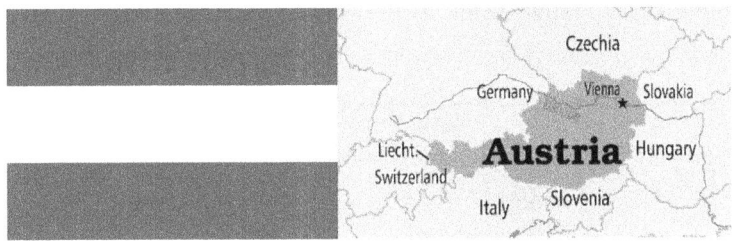

Look to me, and be saved, all the ends of the earth; for I am God, and there is no one else.
— Isaiah 45:22 WEB

Majestic God, the One who alone saves, I stand as an intercessor for Austria and cry out that hearts in Vienna and throughout the alpine valleys will look to You and find true salvation. I declare that where people hold to cultural faith or long-standing religious form without knowing the living Christ, Your Spirit will pierce through ritual and habit. Let those who have been disillusioned by institutional failures encounter the living Savior in fresh, personal ways. Where many believe in God but not in Jesus, bring clear revelation of Christ's person and work.

Lord, You know the beauty of Austria's culture—music, art, poetry—and I pray that these gifts become avenues of grace rather than mere heritage. Breathe revival into young people and prayer movements; multiply the seed that began the Austrian Prayer Congress into a movement across schools, universities, and workplaces. Where Catholic identity has become a default, send renewal that honors legitimate traditions while awakening hearts to a transformative relationship with Jesus. Raise a generation of evangelical and charismatic congregations that grow strong in discipleship, compassion, and doctrinal clarity.

Heavenly Father, heal wounds caused by scandal and institutional distrust. Raise leaders of integrity who will shepherd with humility and justice, and who will actively pursue reconciliation with those harmed. Let the renewal movements within the churches produce a genuine hunger for holiness and for public witness that is winsome and wise. Multiply indigenous expressions of worship, creative arts, and outreach that make the gospel accessible to Austrians who currently do not seek God outside the Church.

Lord of nations, I prophesy multiplication of faithful congregations, especially those that honor and proclaim Jesus. Let the 0.5% evangelical minority not remain small but become a catalytic presence for widespread spiritual awakening. May Austria be a place where culture and Christ collide for revival, where the lost look to You and are saved. In Jesus' name, Amen.

14

Azerbaijan

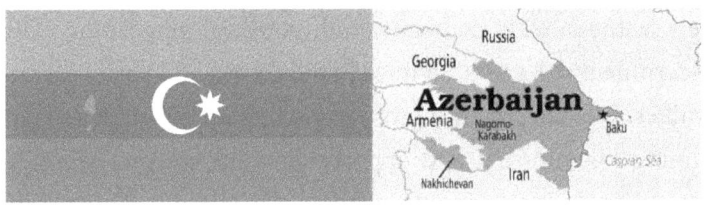

> Behold, how good and how pleasant it is for brothers to dwell together in unity!
> — Psalm 133:1 WEB

Sovereign God of peace, I take my place as a fervent intercessor for Azerbaijan and declare that unity among believers will emerge as a fragrant offering before Your throne. I address You as the Builder of every fellowship and ask that the seeds You have planted among Azeri believers—birthed under trial and watered by perseverance—would blossom into authentic unity. Where believers are scattered across ethnic lines and where many followers are of foreign origin, bind them together with cords of love and mutual respect that cannot be broken.

Heavenly Father, I pray for bold fellowship in Baku and beyond: let foreign-born and indigenous Christians find common language in worship, poetry, music, and indigenous forms of praise that honor both culture and Christ. Give the local church wisdom to disciple converts deeply, to protect vulnerable communities, and to create safe spaces for spiritual growth. Strengthen small groups, house churches, and ministries that encourage believers to bear one another's burdens, confess sin, and rejoice together in the power of the resurrection.

Lord Jesus, where believers once numbered only a few, multiply their witness with courage amid potential opposition. Grant discernment to leaders, courage to the young, and perseverance to families. Provide practical provision—literature in native tongues, training for ministry, and opportunities for creative evangelism that respect local norms while proclaiming Christ. Bring reconciliation where suspicion exists and grant those who follow You influence in neighborhoods, workplaces, and homes through lives marked by integrity and love.

Almighty Shepherd, I declare that Azerbaijan will see strengthening of fellowship, deeper indigenous expressions of faith, and flourishing unity that testifies to the reconciling power of Jesus. May the church there become a light that draws many to salvation and to communal life that is both good and pleasant before You. In Jesus' name, Amen.

15

The Bahamas

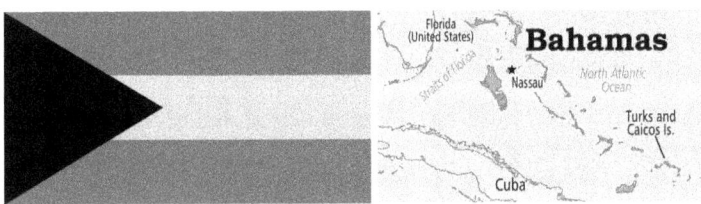

He has told you, humanity, what is good; and what does the LORD require of you, but to do justice, and to love kindness, and to walk humbly with your God?
— Micah 6:8 WEB

Righteous Judge and compassionate Father, I come with a prophetic burden for The Bahamas and call forth a people and a government who will do justice, love kindness, and walk humbly with You. I declare that the islands—Nassau and every shore—belong to Your gracious rule, and I ask for a moral awakening that repudiates materialism and elevates humility and neighborly love over consumer excess. Where tourism-driven wealth has skewed values and where inequality wounds communities, send leaders with a heart for the poor, policies that protect the vulnerable, and a church that embodies sacrificial generosity.

Lord God, bend the hearts of those who hold economic power to steward resources for the common good. Break the power of corruption, tax havens that harm local opportunity, and practices that create parallel worlds of wealth and poverty. Raise public servants who pursue social righteousness, criminal justice reforms that heal rather than only punish, and community programs that address root causes of violence, drugs, and family breakdown. Let ministry among Haitian immigrants and the poorest communities be strong, practical, and full of dignity.

Merciful Savior, raise up churches and believers who model kindness and hospitality in tangible ways: mentoring youth, supporting single parents, restoring families, and offering employment training. Replace transactional religiosity with incarnational ministry that meets needs and points people to Christ. Use the high literacy and strong Christian identity to mobilize compassionate civic engagement and gospel-driven social enterprise that provides pathways out of poverty.

King of Glory, I prophesy a Bahamian renaissance of conscience and mercy: a nation where justice flows like a river, kindness is daily practice, and humility before God shapes public life. Let the Church lead in reconciliation and social transformation, and may the islands reflect Your kingdom rule in every harbor and home. In Jesus' name, Amen.

16

Bahrain

> Ask of me, and I will give you the nations for your inheritance, and the ends of the earth for your possession.
> — Psalm 2:8 WEB

Sovereign King, Lord of hosts and Lover of the nations, I come boldly before Your throne as a prophet-prayer for Bahrain. I declare Your good rule over Manama and every city and shoreline of this island kingdom. I lift up the freedom that has been granted here and ask, by the authority of Christ, that those freedoms become avenues for gospel advance and kingdom harvest. I ask You, O God, to give Bahrain as an inheritance to Your people: let Your rule be recognized in the halls of influence, the marketplaces frequented by visitors from Saudi Arabia and Kuwait, and in the quiet homes where believers gather.

Father, I intercede for the 9.8% who acknowledge Christ and for the 2.9% who are evangelical—strengthen them. I pray for unity among established churches and the informal networks that meet in homes and small gatherings. Bind them together by the Spirit; let humility, discernment, and sacrificial love replace rivalry. Let their testimony be a bright light to the many expatriates and visiting Saudis and Kuwaitis who come seeking rest and relief; may every conversation, act of kindness, and public worship be a spiritual bridge that opens hearts to Jesus.

Lord Jesus, raise up bold, wise, and holy leaders from within Bahrain's Christian community—leaders who will disciple, protect, and steward the high literacy and urban opportunity to plant deeper roots of faith. Where 47% remain unevangelized, send evangelistic favor and divine appointments. Let the gospel enter homes, markets, universities and ministries to the marginalized, turning casual freedom into committed worship and cultural transformation.

Holy Spirit, we call heaven's strategies into the nation: open doors for cooperation with Arab neighbors, bring reconciliation where suspicion exists, and reveal Christ to those who have never heard. Let Bahrain become a spiritual hub from which the gospel flows to the Gulf, and let every visitor depart changed by encounter with You. I declare Your kingdom come, Your will be done across Bahrain. In Jesus' name, Amen.

17

BANGLADESH

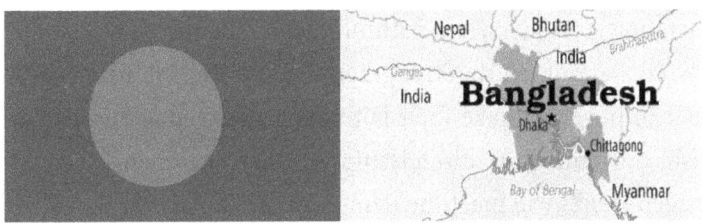

Blessed is the nation whose God is the LORD; the people he has chosen for his own inheritance.
— Psalm 33:12 WEB

Almighty God, Rock of Ages and Redeemer of nations, I stand in the breach for Bangladesh. I cry out that the blessedness You promise to a people whose God is the LORD would come upon Dhaka, Chattogram, Sylhet and every riverside village. I claim Your blessing over a nation battered by floods, poverty, and political upheaval; I call heaven's mercy to break the cycles that have kept millions in want. I ask You to make Bangladesh a people known for depending upon and honoring You, so that the name of the LORD becomes a shelter and strength.

Father, You see the suffering of the poor, the displacement after each rising river season, and the lack of full-time ministers and trained leaders. I pray for structural transformation: give godly solutions for jobs, for agricultural resilience, for flood mitigation—bring wisdom to interim leaders and those who govern so they will enact just policies that lift the poor and protect the vulnerable. Where governance has failed, send integrity, bold reformers, and processes that heal rather than inflame. Bring peace to the streets and stability to families.

Lord Jesus, raise up leaders for the churches—mature pastors, discipling lay leaders, and faithful teacher-shepherds who will root new converts in truth. Strengthen the few Bengali believers who labor in poverty; make their faith deep and contagious. Release a fresh movement of discipleship so that the many unreached Bengali hearts will meet the living Christ. Replace weak faith with bold witness, and foster spiritual community that bears persecution with grace.

Holy Spirit, move across the cultural and religious tapestry—among Sufi-influenced Muslims, Hindu families, and unreached groups—revealing the living Savior through dreams, mercy, and gospel proclamation. I pray for revival that is both supernatural and practical: churches equipped to feed, to teach, and to heal land and soul. Let Bangladesh be counted among the nations that bless the LORD with visible fruit. In Jesus' name, Amen.

18

BARBADOS

> If my people, who are called by my name, will humble themselves, and pray and seek my face, and turn from their wicked ways; then I will hear from heaven, and will forgive their sin, and will heal their land.
> — 2 Chronicles 7:14 WEB

Sovereign Lord, King of Glory, I stand in prayer over Barbados and plead for a Spirit-led awakening among your sons and daughters there. I declare that the land which has long professed Christ will know the reality of His lordship again. I call the Church in Bridgetown and across the parishes to genuine repentance, heartfelt humility, and passionate pursuit of Your face. Let confession replace complacency; let commitment replace casual profession. I ask that where materialism and theological drift have taken root, Your refining fire would restore true devotion.

Father, bless the 94.9% who identify as Christian with the power of conversion—not mere affiliation, but transformed lives marked by obedience, holiness, and sacrificial love. Strengthen the 34.2% evangelical witness to lead by example: deepen preaching, awaken small groups, and cultivate robust discipleship so that children and youth (17% under fifteen) inherit a living faith rather than a cultural religion. Drive out the love of wealth that crowds out devotion and renew a hunger for your Word and presence.

Lord Jesus, counter the rise in violence and moral decline with the Gospel's reconciling and restraining power. Empower churches to be centers of restoration—to minister to families, to rehabilitate broken lives, and to offer hope to those ensnared by crime. Let theological clarity return, and let congregations rediscover scripture as their authority, not cultural trends. Raise up ministers and lay leaders who preach Christ crucified and risen.

Holy Spirit, bring revival that transforms Sunday worship into week-long witness. Let Barbados be a light in the Caribbean: a people renewed, a society healed, and a nation that models the beauty of Christ's reign. I ask that every temple of commerce, every school, and every home bows to Your sovereign rule. In Jesus' name, Amen.

19

BELARUS

> Give justice to the weak and the fatherless; maintain the right of the afflicted and destitute. Rescue the weak and the poor; deliver them from the hand of the wicked.
> — Psalm 82:3–4 WEB

Sovereign Judge, Lord of righteousness, I come before You on behalf of Belarus, and I demand the outworking of Your justice across Minsk and every province. I call for the rights of the weak and the fatherless to be vindicated; I ask You to expose corruption and the hidden systems that keep people oppressed. Where authoritarian control has silenced the people and where sham processes have obscured truth, bring illumination, accountability, and the rule of law that reflects Your heart for justice.

Father, I pray for the weary and those who have lost hope under an ineffective centralized economy. Release creative wisdom for economic renewal; bring honest leaders who will steward resources for the flourishing of families, not personal enrichment. Let the support that once came from external powers be reoriented into opportunities that lift ordinary citizens. Give courage to reformers, and protect whistleblowers and truth-tellers from harm.

Lord Jesus, visit Your church in Belarus with courage, unity, and compassion. Strengthen believers who have become discouraged, and give them boldness to serve the poor, the displaced, and those traumatized by political unrest. Let the Church be a place where justice and mercy meet: where legal aid, reconciliation ministries, and practical assistance demonstrate the gospel. Soften hearts that cling to power; open doors for repentance and national healing.

Holy Spirit, bring a fresh spring of hope that replaces fear. Let propaganda fall away before truth; let mercy and accountability walk hand in hand. I petition You for a brighter future—for restored dignity, for bread on the table, and for leaders who fear You and lead with integrity. May Belarus experience a sovereign turnaround under Your rule. In Jesus' name, Amen.

20

BELGIUM

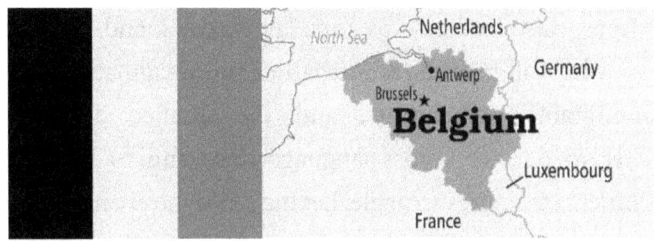

> Peace be within your walls, and prosperity within your palaces. For my brothers' and companions' sakes, I will now say, "Peace be within you."
> — Psalms 122:7-8 WEB

Lord of Peace, Prince of Unity, I lift Brussels, Wallonia, Flanders and every community of Belgium into Your hands. I declare that Your joy and pleasantness will come where division and suspicion now sit. I pray that language and cultural fault-lines between Flemish and Walloon, and the tensions of many newcomer communities, will be bridged by the reconciling power of the gospel. Let the Church model a unity that flows from shared faith, humility, and mutual service—a unity that nations see and are drawn to.

Father, strengthen those who are faithful in a land drifting toward secularism. Where attendance has waned and the Bible has been neglected, pour out a renewed hunger for Your Word; let the Bible societies' work bear fruit as Scripture takes deep root in homes and hearts. Reverse the trend of theological hollowing; revive preaching that proclaims Christ's lordship and practical discipleship that transforms families and public life.

Lord Jesus, raise leaders—pastors, lay workers, and marketplace saints—who will pursue reconciliation and imaginative outreach to immigrants, unbelievers, and the disaffected. Empower churches to partner across language lines and to serve where government structures struggle. Let the 31% who are non-religious encounter the living God through acts of mercy, honest witness, and miracles that accompany the gospel.

Holy Spirit, breathe fresh life into Belgium's civic spaces: wisdom for leaders, humility in debate, and policies that protect the vulnerable while honoring truth. May the Church be an instrument of healing so that Belgian society can rediscover the beauty of unity in Christ. I ask that Your kingdom come and Your will be done across this land. In Jesus' name, Amen.

21

Belize

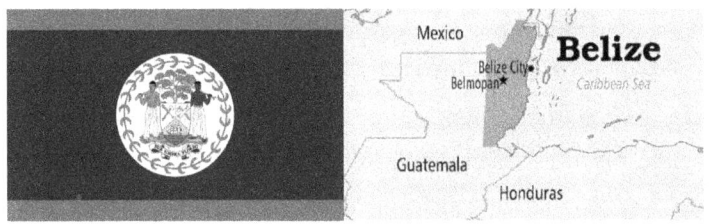

> "If they sin against you (for there is no man who doesn't sin), and you are angry with them… if they return to you with all their heart and with all their soul in the land of their captivity…then hear from heaven, even from your dwelling place, their prayer and their petitions, and maintain their cause, and forgive your people who have sinned against you.
> — 2 Chronicles 6:36-39 WEB

Almighty King of nations, Ancient of Days, I stand before Your throne for Belize with a prophetic voice: humble the heart of this people and draw them to Your face. You hear the cry of nations and answer repentance with restoration. I declare that where attendance has become casual and religion a habit, Your Spirit will move to awaken hunger for truth, bringing genuine encounters with Jesus that cut through syncretism and superstition. Let those who speak Spanish, Kriol, Mayan tongues,

Garifuna voices, and English hear one clear Gospel message that removes confusion and exposes every false hold of black magic or pagan practice.

Lord Jesus, Builder of Your Church, breathe revival into Belmopan, Belize City, and every village and shore. Raise up culturally sensitive witnesses who can carry the gospel with compassion and humility—missionaries, pastors, teachers, and ordinary believers who understand how to speak the truth in love. As the people humble themselves, raise a generation of learners who will seek Your face rather than cling to inherited errors. Empower discipleship that teaches solid doctrine and fosters transformed lifestyles, so the outward appearance of religion gives way to inward obedience and love.

Righteous Judge and Tender Shepherd, intervene in the families and communities where mixed beliefs cause fragmentation. Replace fear with faith, superstition with revelation, and the authority of Christ over every occult influence. Give church leaders courage to preach repentance and mercy, and give congregations boldness to demonstrate compassion—hospitality to immigrants, restoration to the marginalized, and healing for hearts bound by sin. Let the literacy and openness of Belize be harnessed to spread Scripture in ways people can grasp, applying the truth to work, culture, and everyday living.

Sovereign Lord, release healing to the land as hearts turn to You. Make Belize a place where the Kingdom comes—justice, mercy, humility, and worship—not merely ritual. Raise up prayer movements, house churches, and outreaches that bridge language and culture. Let the 2% unreached be found, and let the 10% who attend church become the salt and light that transforms neighborhoods. We declare a great harvest of souls, a cleansing of errors, and a church marked by holiness and love. In Jesus' name, Amen.

22

BENIN

Learn to do good; seek justice, reprove the oppressor; defend the fatherless, plead for the widow.
— Isaiah 1:17 WEB

Sovereign Lord, Judge of the nations, we cry out for Benin: let righteousness and justice sweep through her cities, towns, and borders. Where illegal economies and trafficking have shadowed the lives of children and the vulnerable, bring forth Your clarifying light. May the hidden networks that prey upon the young be exposed, dismantled, and replaced by systems of protection and community care. Call forth government leaders, law enforcement, and civic servants who will pursue justice with integrity, and give them wisdom to partner with godly nations and ministries for restoration and protection.

Compassionate Father, stir the hearts of Your people in Benin to defend the fatherless and plead the cause of widows and victims.

Raise up churches and believers who will not be silent: let them open shelters, create safe corridors for exploited children, and work with international agencies to stop the trafficking pathways. Where Nigeria's influence has been a mixed force, release angels of discernment to redirect economic ties toward godly trade and upliftment. Teach communities to convert informal markets into lawful, dignified livelihoods that honor labor and human dignity.

Lord of the harvest, despite great need, you have given Benin a spiritual receptivity—let that openness become a door for the gospel to reach Muslim peoples and isolated communities. Empower evangelists who understand local languages and cultures; bless training programs that increase literacy and Bible access; translate Scripture into more tongues. Raise a new generation of leaders and teachers who will disciple converts into sturdy, morally grounded followers of Christ so the seed of faith grows into a harvest of transformed families and neighborhoods.

King of all, I prophesy a turning in Benin: corruption will lose ground, trafficking rings will crumble, and justice will become the norm. Let benevolent partnerships flourish and let the Church be a sanctuary of restoration. From Cotonou to the smallest village, breathe life into the weak and courage into the faithful until Benin reflects Your justice and mercy across West Africa. In Jesus' name, Amen.

23

Bermuda

> Pure and undefiled religion before God and the Father is this: to visit the fatherless and the widows in their affliction, and to keep himself unspotted from the world.
> — James 1:27 WEB

King of Glory, I lift Bermuda before you—this island of beauty and heritage that knows the name of Christ yet so often worships form over fire. Father, awaken the Church from comfortable rituals and surface religiosity. Let worship become a spring of holiness that flows into daily life, so that the island's high literacy and strong Christian heritage are matched by integrity, compassion, and sacrificial love. Replace performance with intimacy; replace appearances with authenticity; let devotion here be lived, not merely displayed.

Lord Jesus, refine the hearts of leaders and congregations across Hamilton and every parish. Give pastors courage to preach truth that convicts and heals; give congregants the grace to be vulnerable and repentant. Where the outward show has eclipsed inward transformation, send revival—conviction that leads to real change: marriages healed, addictions broken, finances stewarded, and public virtue restored. Let the wealthy and influential use their power for justice and mercy, investing in programs that visit the fatherless, support the widows, and serve the poor.

Holy Spirit, cultivate communities that are unspotted from the world—churches that are living testimonies of Christ's kingdom. Inspire youth movements that reject hypocrisy and pursue holiness, and equip worshippers to be city and island changers in business, law, education, and family life. Strengthen small groups, discipleship, and outreach so faith is passed on authentically and deeply, not merely culturally.

Prince of Peace, I declare Bermuda reclaimed for genuine spirituality: let your Kingdom rule bring humility, charity, and a flame of faithful witness that cannot be contained by mere tradition. Let the 1% unevangelized and those who attend in form only encounter the living Christ in ways that alter their lives permanently. Raise a people whose lives reflect heaven—and in doing so, let the island shine as a beacon of true Christianity in the region. In Jesus' name, Amen.

24

BHUTAN

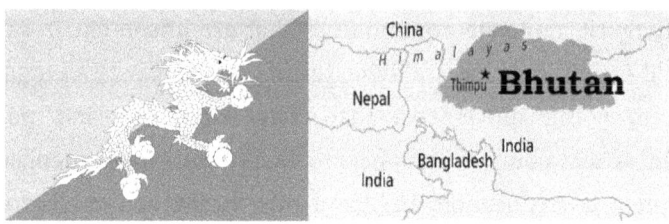

> How then shall they call on him in whom they have not believed? How shall they believe in him of whom they have not heard? How shall they hear without a preacher?
> — Romans 10:14 WEB

Lord of the harvest, Master of every tongue and tribe, I cry aloud for Bhutan—the secluded kingdom of mountains and monasteries. Break the chains of isolation and displace the strongholds of Vajrayana Buddhism and Bon that have held souls captive. Send forth preachers, translators, and gentle witnesses into every Dzongkha- and Nepali-speaking valley, into the hearts of Dzongkha, Tshangla, Lepcha, Kheng, Gurung peoples and beyond. Where Scriptures are absent, provide them; where language barriers exist, raise faithful translators to bring the Word into living speech.

Sovereign King, touch King Wangchuk and the royal family with the love and power of Jesus; soften hearts at the highest levels so policies that currently limit spiritual freedom are turned toward open skies for the Gospel. Let the rigidity of isolation be replaced with compassionate hospitality toward the Good News. Raise Bhutanese believers—simple, steadfast witnesses who embody Christ's humility and courage—who will share the gospel face-to-face in culturally wise and respectful ways, planting seeds that bring life.

Holy Spirit, confront the occult and demonic influence rooted in indigenous systems; displace fear with the presence of Christ and the authority of the cross. Let hidden places yield to light; let spiritual bondage loosen its grip and leave communities transformed. Empower the small number of existing Christians to become bold evangelists and compassionate servants, showing the love of Christ through healing, education, and acts of mercy that meet practical needs and open hearts.

Father, I declare a new season in Bhutan where hearing begets believing, and believing begets calling on the name of Jesus. Let Scripture flood the languages of the Himalayas; let worship rise in countless valleys; let families be reconciled and tribal enmities heal. We claim a movement of God among the least reached—converts, communities, and leaders saved and sanctified—so Bhutan may know spiritual freedom and the Kingdom come. In Jesus' name, Amen.

25

Bolivia

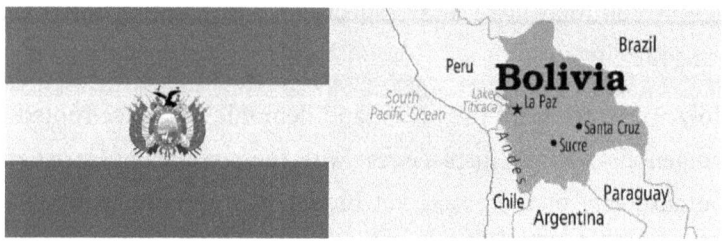

> He has showed you, O man, what is good; and what does the LORD require of you, but to do justice, and to love kindness, and to walk humbly with your God?
> — Micah 6:8 WEB

Lord of justice and mercy, I lift Bolivia before Your throne in the midst of its valleys, highlands, and plains. Where poverty and inequality have hardened hearts and divided peoples, raise a generation who will do justice and love kindness. Displace the greed that elevates coca over honest labor; transform the markets so families no longer feel compelled to choose illegal crops for survival. Give leaders in the east and west, in urban centers and rural communities, wisdom and courage to pursue policies that reduce injustice and steward natural resources for the common good.

Mighty Redeemer, speak into the tensions between indigenous, mixed, and elite groups. Heal ethnic wounds, right historical wrongs, and bind the nation together in a shared pursuit of righteousness. Equip evangelical leaders—not merely as political actors, but as servants of the poor—to deepen discipleship, teach sound doctrine, and demonstrate moral integrity. Raise up thousands of leaders who are formed by Scripture and humility, who will resist false teaching and personal compromise, and who will lead institutions of education, health, and social service with Kingdom values.

Healer and Provider, send practical interventions: sustainable agriculture, fair trade alternatives to coca, education that lifts literacy and opportunity, and community programs that protect children and restore dignity. Let the Church mobilize for compassionate justice—legal aid, microloans, vocational training—so the poor receive both gospel truth and tangible hope. Convert spiritual fervor into disciplined discipleship that produces fruit: servants who care for the needy, speak truth to power, and model integrity.

Sovereign Lord, I prophesy that Bolivia will be a place where Your will is increasingly done—where politicians, pastors, and people act in ways that reflect heaven's order. Let moral clarity emerge, corruption lose its grip, and the Church become a catalytic force for reconciliation and uplift. Raise up the new leaders You promised: courageous, wise, and humble servants who will transform the nation for Your glory. In Jesus' name, Amen.

26

BOSNIA AND HERZEGOVINA

> For he himself is our peace, who made both groups one, and broke down the middle wall of partition, the hostility.
> — Ephesians 2:14 WEB

Sovereign Lord, Prince of Peace, I stand in the gap for Bosnia and Herzegovina and declare Your peace that surpasses human repair over Sarajevo, Mostar, Banja Luka and every valley and mountain between. I come before Your throne as a prophetic intercessor, calling down the power that unites—dismantle every stronghold of hatred and ethnic hostility that still lingers from past violence. Let the dividing walls built by fear, anger, and grief be broken in the name of Jesus so that former enemies might be made one in heart and purpose under Your reign.

Holy Judge and Compassionate Healer, breathe new life into families and communities who have carried wounds for decades. Where citizens have been scattered, encourage return and reconciliation; where scars have hardened into tribal identity, soften hearts so forgiveness can grow. Bring clarity and conviction to those who traffick in organized crime; expose networks that profit from suffering and bring lawful, godly justice to their operations. Raise honest leaders who will refuse bribes, reform systems, and steward resources for the common good. Let the nation's high literacy be a conduit for truth and reconstruction of character so rebuilding is not only physical, but moral and spiritual.

Lord of the Nations, turn the minds and hearts of the youth who are tempted to leave into a new generation that chooses to stay, to deepen roots, and to lead. Ignite campuses and neighborhoods with movements of young believers who will bring entrepreneurial vision, sound governance, and courageous witness. Let the churches—across Bosnian, Serbian, and Croatian languages—be agents of bridge-building, where worship, service, and honest repentance produce communities marked by justice, mercy, and peace. Give pastors prophetic courage to preach unity without compromising truth and to disciple people into lives of civic responsibility.

Heavenly King, I prophesy that Bosnia will know a fresh season of reconciliation under Your banner. Let the Gospel break every chain of bitterness, let schools and civil institutions rise in integrity, and let crime give way to flourishing towns where families taste hope. Bind together once-divided hearts by the reconciling love of Christ until the land reflects heaven's unity. In Jesus' name, Amen.

27

Botswana

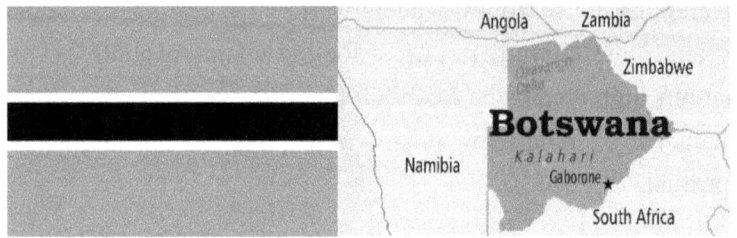

> By justice a king establishes the land; by righteousness he establishes it.
> — Proverbs 29:4 WEB

Majestic King, Architect of nations, I lift Botswana before You with thanksgiving and a prophetic plea: let righteousness establish this land and let justice be the firm foundation for Vision 2036. I declare that the peaceful transfer of power and the stability this nation enjoys will not be merely a political footnote but the soil in which Kingdom fruit grows. Bless the new leaders with God-given wisdom, humility, and integrity so that policy and practice honor the common good and reflect Your heart for the poor and the vulnerable.

Lord of Wisdom, pour out discernment on those shaping Vision 2036 so that prosperity for all becomes a reality under Christ's lordship. Protect the gains made against corruption and raise up honest administrators, judges, and civil servants who choose service over self. Let Botswana's strong urban centers and growing youth population be windows of opportunity: invest in education, apprenticeships, and spiritual formation so the 33.8% who are under fifteen do not become a statistic but a generation of kingdom-minded leaders.

Compassionate Shepherd, empower the Church across English and Setswana communities to partner in social transformation—advocating for sustainable environment practices, human development, and peace. Raise evangelists and disciples who model practical mercy: feeding programs that honor dignity, environmental stewardship that sustains the bush and ranch, and community projects that restore hope. Let the comparatively low unreached percentage be burned into zeal—send fresh missionaries into the 4% unevangelized places and into urban margins where spiritual need remains hidden beneath prosperity.

Sovereign Lord, I prophesy stability transmuted into flourishing: where justice reigns, poverty yields; where righteousness leads, corruption flees. Make Botswana a testimony to what a nation looks like when Your principles govern society. Let the name of Jesus be honored in government halls, marketplaces, and family tables so that Vision 2036 becomes Vision of the Kingdom realized on earth. In Jesus' name, Amen.

28

BRAZIL

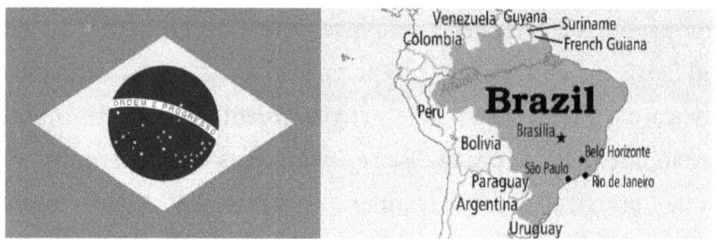

I in them, and you in me, that they may be made perfect in one; and that the world may know that you sent me, and loved them, even as you loved me.
— John 17:23 WEB

Sovereign Lord and Lover of Brazil, I take my stand as a prophetic voice for this vast nation—from the favelas of Rio and São Paulo to the rivers of the Amazon—and declare that Your unity and love will overcome division and pain. Shine the light of Your reconciling presence into every polarized space where political rage and ideological hatred have set neighbors against one another. Let the evangelical fervor that prays in plazas and stadiums be united in humility and truth, guided by grace, discerning spirit, and sacrificial love rather than partisan zeal.

Lord Jesus, Builder of the Church, raise up leaders—pastors, lay leaders, women's networks, and youth movements—who will translate powerful prayer into sustained discipleship and social action. Send faithful church planters into the northeast and the Amazon where spiritual and physical needs run deep. Break the chains of poverty, child labor, and exploitation: mobilize churches to rescue and restore children trapped in forced labor and prostitution, to mentor youth, and to offer vocational pathways that honor dignity and break cycles of poverty.

Righteous Judge, bring justice to the Amazon and protection to indigenous communities crushed by illegal deforestation and exploitation. Move the hearts of those with power and influence toward sustainable practices that steward creation and uphold indigenous rights. Empower Christian advocates to stand with the oppressed, to lobby for fair laws, and to offer alternatives to destructive economic gains. In the slums where violence and gang rule scar daily life, let community churches become hubs of refuge, education, and reconciliation—bridging police, public services, and neighbors in mercy-driven initiatives.

Holy Spirit, weave diversity into strength across Brazil's many people groups and languages. Let the 36,000 unreached Amazon communities meet Christ through missionary boats, compassionate relief, and culturally sensitive witness. Pour out renewal on the millions who call Jesus Lord so they become practical agents of justice, peacemakers, and defenders of the poor. I prophesy a Brazil where the Church moves beyond ceremony into courageous, redemptive action—where the Kingdom reigns in policy, economy, and everyday life. In Jesus' name, Amen.

29

BRITISH VIRGIN ISLANDS

> You are the light of the world. A city set on a hill cannot be hidden.
> — Matthew 5:14 WEB

O Lord of light and mercy, I lift the British Virgin Islands before Your throne and declare that this island nation shall shine with the true radiance of Christ. Where tourism and offshore finance bring temptation and moral erosion, raise a holy remnant who will carry Your light into marinas, resorts, and markets. Let the 84.9% who claim Christianity move beyond cultural identity to embodied discipleship, living visibly as a city set on a hill—unashamed, holy, generous, and hospitable to both visitors and immigrants.

Heavenly Father, empower local churches and ministries to be the first responders to moral and social shifts. Equip believers to meet tourists and newcomers with love and truth: gospel conversations shaped by compassion, services for the vulnerable, and outreach that offers hope rather than judgment. Where illegal immigrants arrive with mixed motives, give wisdom to authorities and grace to communities to protect the innocent and extend pathways to legitimate employment and care. Let Christian witness be wise, welcoming, and redemptive.

Sustainer of every island, raise up prophetic and pastoral leadership that models integrity in business and governance. Bless educators, judges, and leaders to steward resources ethically, and let high literacy and access to education translate into movements of justice and mercy. Mobilize youth and evangelical networks to lead in social service—mentoring, anti-exploitation efforts, and family support—so the pleasure-seeking culture is met with kingdom alternatives that dignify individuals and heal relationships.

Good Shepherd, I prophesy renewal over the British Virgin Islands: where tourism once threatened shallow living, deepen faith; where offshore finance tempted compromise, establish righteous practice; where immigrants arrived in need, provide protection and hope. Let the islands become a beacon—small in size, great in testimony—a visible city on a hill whose light draws many to the Savior. In Jesus' name, Amen.

30

Brunei

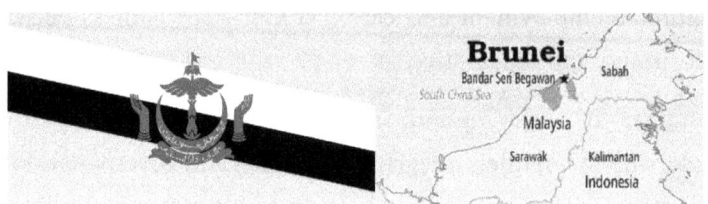

> For God has not given us a spirit of fear, but of power, and of love, and of sound mind.
> — 2 Timothy 1:7 WEB

Almighty God, King over kings, I intercede for Brunei and declare Your sovereign protection over believers in the midst of pressure and secrecy. Break the spirit of fear that would silence witness and replace it with Your spirit of power, love, and self-discipline. Though the nation practices conservative Islam and laws restrict open evangelism, I call forth a courageous, wise Church that walks in boldness tempered by prudence—serving the poor, healing the sick, and embodying gospel love in ways that cannot be ignored.

Lord of Freedom, move in the hearts of the royal family and leaders—soften their understanding, open their eyes to the beauty of Christ's love, and grant spiritual hunger to those in authority.

Where monitoring and constraint create hidden discipleship, bless those secret gatherings with deep spiritual formation, sound teaching, and unity. Give converts from minority groups and any within the palace family protection, clarity, and the peace that passes understanding. Strengthen families, house churches, and Christian workers with wisdom to navigate laws while remaining faithful.

Sovereign Protector, raise a generation in Brunei who will stand with love and discernment—champions of religious freedom, advocates for human dignity, and servants to those in need. Provide creative, lawful avenues for Scripture distribution where permitted and unconventional channels of compassion—schools, clinics, and social services—that display the gospel through acts. Break spiritual strongholds of legalism and fear, and replace them with communities of believers who reflect Christ's power, sacrificial love, and sound minds.

Heavenly Father, I prophesy that Brunei will not be left in spiritual darkness: Your power will embolden the faithful; Your love will win hearts; Your sound mind will guide strategy. Let the Church grow quietly but surely until openness increases and freedom for proclamation rises. May the day come when Bruneians from every background worship openly and their nation becomes a place of transformed lives under the Lordship of Jesus. In Jesus' name, Amen.

31

BULGARIA

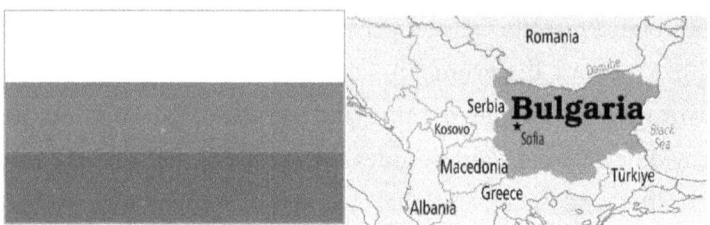

Mercy and truth have met together; righteousness and peace have kissed.
— Psalm 85:10 WEB

Sovereign Lord, Rock of Ages, I come before You as a bold intercessor for Bulgaria, lifting Sofia and every town steeped in memory and sorrow. I declare Your mercy to this nation and call for a fresh outbreak of truth to dismantle lies that have settled into the systems of life. Where communism once severed faith, where corruption and crime networks still prey on the weak, I ask that righteousness rise like a tide and make crooked places straight. Let the land be healed where grievances hardened into identity, and let peace flow through streets, workplaces, and homes that have known too much unrest.

Father of compassion, breathe life into churches and believers so that their profession of Christianity becomes visible compassion and costly love. Give pastors prophetic courage to preach holiness and the beauty of life, to teach young couples about covenant and the dignity of children, and to lead with moral clarity in a society grappling with abortion and broken marriages. Strengthen discipleship so that the 1.9% evangelical remnant becomes a multiplying witness—teaching Scripture, modeling restoration, and demonstrating God's grace in neighborhoods, schools, and hospitals. May literacy and intellect serve kingdom formation, turning learned minds toward wisdom and service.

Lord of the nations, confront the spirit of departure among youth and replace their desire to emigrate with purpose and hope. Inspire economic creativity and policies grounded in justice so that young Bulgarians see their future at home; stir entrepreneurs, educators, and church-led initiatives to provide meaningful work and training. Break the power of organized crime and expose networks that rob communities of safety; give judges, police, and leaders integrity and the courage to reform systems so poverty does not become a perpetual cycle.

Heavenly King, I prophesy a Bulgaria renewed: a nation where mercy meets truth visibly—where families are healed, where young people choose to build rather than flee, where the Church is a reconciling and restorative force in public life. Multiply godly leaders who will steward resources with honesty and lead with humility so that Bulgaria bears witness to Your transforming power across Eastern Europe. In Jesus' name, Amen.

32

BURKINA FASO

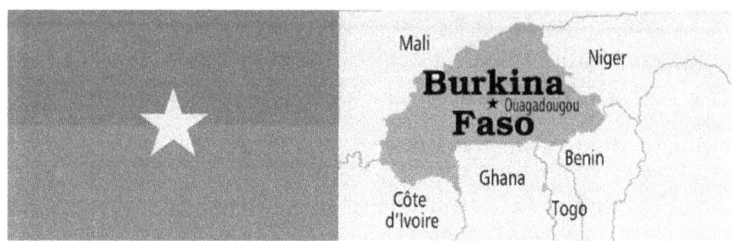

No weapon that is formed against you will prosper; and every tongue that rises against you in judgment you will condemn. This is the heritage of the servants of the LORD, and their righteousness is from me, says the LORD.
— Isaiah 54:17 WEB

Mighty Fortress, Lord who hears the cry of the oppressed, I stand for Burkina Faso and plead that You break the plans of those who traffic in violence and terror. Let plots born of hatred and external influence collapse before Your sovereign hand. Where terrorist cells and trafficking networks seek to terrorize towns and displace families, send Your protection and justice; expose hidden routes, convict hearts that profit from bloodshed, and empower security forces with wisdom and restraint so innocent lives are saved and evil schemes fail.

Compassionate God, pour courage into the hearts of believers and communities who face persecution, fear, and occult influence. Strengthen the small churches with boldness and holiness so that the name of Jesus is carried not in superstition but in demonstrated authority and love. Bless pastors and evangelists with spiritual discernment to confront animism and secret societies with the gospel's transforming power, and with mercy to care for those healed—practical outreach, food security, and trauma counseling that proves Christ's reign.

Sovereign King, equip leaders—military, civic, and community—with godly wisdom to navigate political transitions without plunging the nation into deeper conflict. Soften hardened ethnic tensions by planting programs of reconciliation, shared economic initiatives, and education that honors diversity. Raise up discipleship hubs that increase literacy and offer Scripture in local languages so young people may anchor in truth rather than fear. Let the immense youth demographic be transformed into a generation of peacemakers and nation-builders.

Heavenly Judge and Redeemer, I prophesy restraint over Burkina Faso: coup plots and jihadist ambitions thwarted, trafficking corridors closed, and communities restored to safety. Let the power of Christ break the hold of charms and idols and unleash a movement of holy, fearless love that turns villages into witness centers of Gospel light across the Sahel. In Jesus' name, Amen.

33

BURUNDI

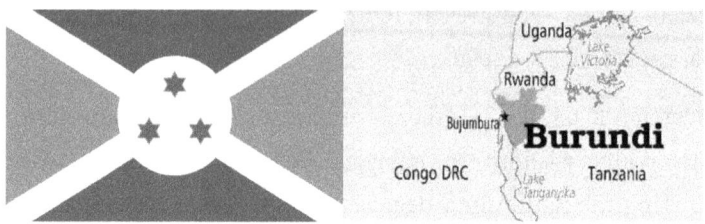

All things are of God, who reconciled us to himself by Jesus Christ, and gave to us the ministry of reconciliation.
— 2 Corinthians 5:18 WEB

God of reconciliation, Author of peace, I lift Burundi—Bujumbura, Gitega, and every hill and valley—before Your throne and claim Your reconciling work over a nation that bears the scars of ethnic strife. I declare that the ministry of reconciliation will arise in this land; where Hutu and Tutsi wounds still ache, let Your Spirit bring true healing that is deeper than political settlements. Make reconciliation a living, practical ministry: neighbors forgiving neighbors, leaders choosing unity over advantage, and communities rebuilding trust through shared service.

Gracious Father, bless the newly elected parliament and stewards of governance in 2025 with humility and wisdom. Give legislators and local leaders eyes to see the long-term good of unity—policies that foster inclusion, transparency, and opportunity for all. Where corruption and poverty threaten stability, raise up godly servants who will steward resources to uplift the poorest, who will invest in education, healthcare, and infrastructure, and who will root out practices that perpetuate inequality.

Healer of broken hearts, bring the gospel into the very places where trauma remains. Strengthen the Church—both historic and evangelical—to be agents of trauma care, reconciliation programs, and vocational training that restore dignity. Empower youth (who make up so large a portion of the population) with education and spiritual formation so they choose to build Burundi rather than flee. Let Christian leaders model sacrificial service and moral integrity so families taste transformed relationships and communities embrace hope.

Lord Jesus, I prophesy a Burundi where the ministry of reconciliation bears fruit: healed families, cooperating leaders, and a rising Church that binds wounds with mercy and truth. Let the gospel be the engine of lasting change so poverty, corruption, and fear give way to a resilient nation shaped by justice, compassion, and peace. In Jesus' name, Amen.

34

CABO VERDE

> "You visit the earth and water it; you greatly enrich it. The river of God is full of water; you prepare their grain; for so You have prepared the earth."
> — Psalm 65:9 WEB

Sovereign Lord of seas and soil, I come before Your throne as a bold intercessor for Cabo Verde and I declare that Your provision and abundant enrichment will come to these islands. I stand in the gap over Praia and every atoll and I call for the rains of Your blessing to meet the arid places. Where scarcity has stalked the land—in water, in soil, in economy—I speak restoration: bring systems, wisdom, and supernatural favor that renew the islands' capacity to flourish. Let the name of Jesus be known as the source of wise stewardship and miraculous supply.

Father, give to the leaders of Cabo Verde supernatural counsel and prudence so they will steward scarce resources with integrity and foresight. Replace poor past management with policies of transparency, sustainable water management, rain-capture technologies, and regenerative agriculture. Raise up public servants who prioritize the common good over personal gain and who invite international partners to help build long-term infrastructure—fresh water systems, desalination, soil reclamation—that do not harm the islands but invite life. Teach the people practices that steward resources and create local resilience so that dependence turns to creativity and opportunity.

Lord, breathe revival into the churches so that 94.6% who name Christ will rise as practical agents of mercy. Let evangelicals and mainline congregations work together to minister to families and youth—nearly thirty percent under fifteen—with programs that teach trades, encourage entrepreneurship, and build character. Bless schools and literacy efforts so that the 87% literacy becomes a platform for civic engagement and innovation. Pour out favor on social enterprises that marry faith and work: fisheries managed with care, tourism that honors creation, and small businesses that employ young people.

Holy Spirit, bring a cultural turning toward generosity and mutual care; let communities share resources and wisdom so no family is left destitute. I prophesy that Cabo Verde will become a living testimony of how small nations can steward limited resources with heavenly wisdom, becoming islands of innovation, compassion, and Kingdom economics. May the sea that surrounds them also supply blessing and the hand of God be evident in every recovery.

In Jesus' name, Amen.

35

CAMBODIA

> "For God has not given us a spirit of fear, but of power, and of love, and of a sound mind."
> — 2 Timothy 1:7 WEB

Almighty God, Fountain of freedom and healer of the broken, I stand as a watchman over Cambodia and declare that the spirit of the Lord will replace fear with power, love, and sound judgment across Phnom Penh and the provinces. I lift up the hearts of the Khmer and call for the chains of spiritual darkness, the grip of fear produced by occult practices and brutal history, to be snapped by the authority of Christ. Let the youthful and the elderly alike receive courage to turn from destructive paths into life-affirming communities rooted in love.

Father, breathe boldness into the tiny Christian remnant and grant strategic vision to church leaders so they may bring gospel light into spirit shrines, universities, marketplaces, and broken homes.

Equip pastors and counselors to offer sound mental-health care and trauma healing for survivors of genocide and abuse; infuse rehabilitation centers and orphanages with professionals trained both in trauma-informed care and in the gospel. Reduce the grip of the drug and sex trades by raising up alternative economics—vocational training, microfinance, and ethical employment—that offers hope and dignity to those most vulnerable.

Lord Jesus, break the power of corrupt networks that plunder national resources and restrict freedoms. Let truth rise in the courts and in civic life; raise reform-minded leaders who will dismantle structures that enable exploitation. Empower believers to serve in healthcare, agriculture, fisheries, and education with excellence so the Church becomes a primary contributor to national rehabilitation. Grant mercy to those once complicit in violence, including former Khmer Rouge members, that they may know the fullness of forgiveness, repentance, and reconcile publicly, demonstrating the power of the Gospel to bring peace.

Holy Spirit, release a sweeping movement of reconciliation across ethnic and spiritual divides—families healed, children rescued, communities reconciled. I prophesy that Cambodia will see an awakening in which Christ's light breaks over the dark places, where survivors find restoration, and where churches lead transformative social renewal. From the rice fields to the rivers of the Tonle Sap, let the Kingdom come in power, love, and sound mind.

In Jesus' name, Amen.

36

CAMEROON

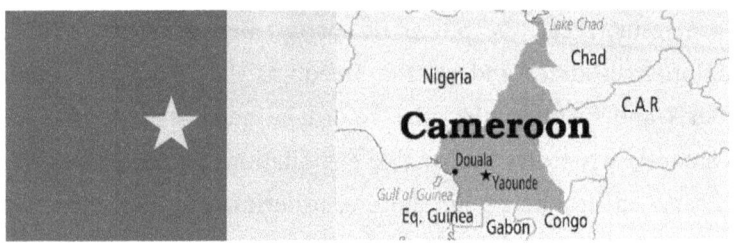

"Righteousness exalts a nation, but sin is a reproach to any people."
— Proverbs 14:34 WEB

Lord of justice and unity, I lift Cameroon before Your throne and declare that righteousness will be exalted across Yaoundé, the English- and French-speaking regions, and into every village where language and faith divide the people. I call heaven's torch upon corruption and its corrupting influence; may the leaders, public servants, and influential citizens be convicted and transformed so that policies and practices reflect fairness rather than theft. Let the culture of tolerance for graft be broken and replaced by a new ethic of accountability, service, and godly stewardship.

Father, raise reconcilers who embody Your wisdom and humility—peacemakers fluent in both French and English, and skilled at bridging cultural and political divides. Empower churches to be centers of reconciliation that deliberately plant joint congregations, inter-linguistic youth programs, and cross-cultural leadership development. Send prophets and pastors to the Anglophone regions whose message is both courageous and compassionate, leading toward dialogue and restoration rather than escalation and revenge. Equip security forces and civil servants to act justly and to protect innocent life rather than deepen division.

Lord Jesus, confront the advance of violent extremism in the north and the spread of separatist tension in the west with an outpouring of protective peace. Let grassroots movements arise that offer education, vocational training, and healthy alternatives to young people so that the nearly half who are under fifteen have hope and constructive pathways. Strengthen Christian leaders in positions of influence—military, police, judiciary—to act with integrity, shield the vulnerable, and bring structures of justice to bear upon those who steal from the nation.

Holy Spirit, pour out unity that crosses language and religion: Christians, Muslims, and traditional communities working side by side for the common good. I prophesy a Cameroon where righteousness releases prosperity, where reconciliation disarms conflict, and where the name of Christ becomes synonymous with peacemaking and honest leadership. Let the Kingdom of God rule in every province and in every heart.

In Jesus' name, Amen.

37

CANADA

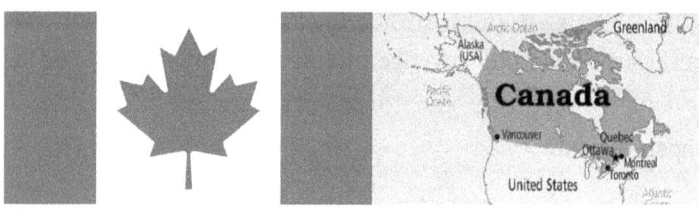

> "I exhort therefore, first of all, that petitions, prayers, intercessions, and giving of thanks be made for all men; for kings and all who are in authority; that we may lead a quiet and peaceable life in all godliness and honesty."
> — 1 Timothy 2:1–2 WEB

Lord of nations and Judge of hearts, I bring Canada before Your throne and declare the lifting of heartfelt prayer for leaders, institutions, and communities across Ottawa and the provinces. I stand in the gap for a nation grappling with spiritual decline, seeking revival in churches that have waned and new expressions of faith that can capture hearts in a secular age. Pour out a fresh hunger for godliness among believers and a wise, winsome witness to those far from You so that society may again experience public life shaped by grace.

Father, pour repentance and renewal into denominations and congregations that have become inward-looking or institutionally rigid. Raise movements of discipleship that equip laypeople to live faith fully in workplaces, schools, and public service. Bless initiatives that prioritize loving witness over partisan agendas, so that Christians demonstrate the Gospel through tangible compassion and truthful speech. Grant revival among mainline churches and multiplication among fresh expressions that resonate with younger generations and diverse immigrant communities.

Lord Jesus, bring healing and reconciliation with Indigenous peoples. Stir a deep and sincere repentance where harm was done, and fashion practical pathways for restitution, culturally-rooted church planting, and leadership development among First Nations. Let the Church partner in addressing poverty, substance abuse, and broken families on reserves, supporting Indigenous-led solutions that honor identity and dignity. Raise advocates who will champion justice, restoration, and meaningful reconciliation.

Holy Spirit, empower believers across Canada to be both humble and bold—servants of mercy who also speak truth in love. I prophesy a Canada where prayer for leaders yields godly governance, where churches multiply in cultural relevance, and where Indigenous and settler communities walk together in restoration. Let the Kingdom come and God's will be done from sea to sea in this land.

In Jesus' name, Amen.

38

CAYMAN ISLANDS

> "The God who made the world and everything in it, he who is Lord of heaven and earth, does not dwell in temples made with hands."
> — Acts 17:24 WEB

Sovereign Creator of seas and islands, I lift the Cayman Islands before Your throne and declare that the God who founded these islands upon the seas will inhabit the hearts of its people and shape public life with His presence. I call a fresh outpouring of worship that moves beyond constitutional mention to incarnational living: churches, neighborhoods, and businesses transformed by the reality that the Lord of heaven and earth personally walks among His people here. May the islands' biblical heritage be more than words but a living testimony of Christ's rule.

Father, empower the ninety-plus churches to be salt and light in every sector—finance, tourism, education, and family life. Where materialism and hedonism tempt prosperity into selfishness, let gospel-minded stewardship prevail. Bless pastors and lay leaders with creativity and courage to disciple congregations for faithful witness in commerce and leisure, producing a culture where success is measured by generosity, character, and service. Let the Biblical heritage on flags and constitutions translate into public policies and daily practices that reflect holiness and joy.

Lord Jesus, stir the youth with a hunger not for mere consumption but for purpose and mission. Multiply evangelical witness and equip believers to welcome visitors and migrants with Christlike hospitality, making the islands a hub for compassionate ministry in the Caribbean. Strengthen Christian influence in civic life so that laws and local ordinances promote family flourishing and protect the vulnerable. Bless the small unevangelized remnant with sensitive outreach that honors cultural identity while bringing life-transforming truth.

Holy Spirit, renew the islands with joy and reverence for Your sovereignty: let worship be both exuberant and humble, let charity flow through tourism and banking, and let the Cayman Islands be a beacon of kingdom economics and godly living. I prophesy communities where faith is evident in deeds, where the seaside declares the Creator's glory, and where outward blessing is matched by inward devotion. May Your reign be plain in every wave that laps the shore.

In Jesus' name, Amen.

39

CENTRAL AFRICAN REPUBLIC

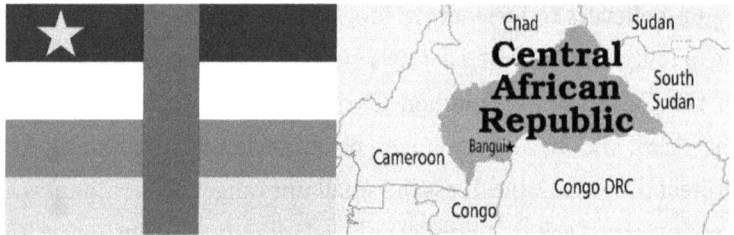

"If my people who are called by my name will humble themselves, and pray, and seek my face, and turn from their wicked ways; then I will hear from heaven, and will forgive their sin, and will heal their land."
— 2 Chronicles 7:14 WEB

Sovereign Lord God of restoration, I come as a burdened watchman and as a voice for the Central African Republic. I declare before Your throne that this nation belongs to You; I call heaven's mercy to meet the desperate cry of her cities and villages. Father, in the name of Jesus I plead for a deep national humbling—let pride and violence be broken, and let repentance like rain fall across Bangui and throughout every province. I refuse to leave this land under the dominion of fear, famine, and fractured communities; I call Your healing and forgiveness to turn her sorrows into songs.

Lord, raise up leaders of integrity and wisdom who will choose life for their people. Where coups, warlords, and militias have trampled justice, send men and women anointed with discernment and courage to bind the violent, disarm the unjust, and rebuild civil structures. Give a spirit of repentance to commanders and chiefs; give them supernatural fear of the Lord that produces honest governance, equitable distribution of resources, and protection for the weak. Multiply strategic workers who will bring training to pastors and send forth missionary students to the unreached regions—especially to the Runga, Sara Kaba, and Gula/Kara peoples—that churches might multiply among both Muslim and animist communities.

Spirit of the living God, heal the wounds of displacement, hunger, and trauma that have scarred whole generations. Let the Church be skilled and fearless in trauma counseling, reconciliation, and practical care. Open pathways for clean water, food security, education and medical outreach so that life and hope replace chronic want. Strengthen believers to stay in rural mission fields and not flee to cities; send revival teams that will endure long-term ministry among those who are most neglected.

I prophesy peace that moves like a river through the Central African Republic: disarming hatred, reconciling former enemies, and planting churches that stand as beacons of justice and mercy. By Your Spirit, build a people who walk in holiness, who love their neighbors, and who show the good news in word and deed until every stronghold falls. In Jesus' name, Amen.

40

CHAD

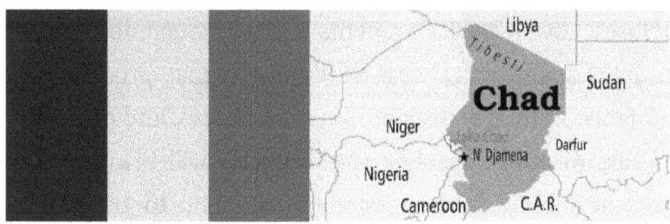

"Blessed is the nation whose God is the LORD; the people he chose for his own inheritance."
— Psalm 33:12 WEB

Majestic King, I lift Chad before Your sovereign throne and decree that this nation is blessed when she is founded upon You. I stand in the gap for N'Djamena and for the scattered towns and refugee camps across the Sahel, calling Your blessing to overshadow hunger, lawlessness, and the chaos of rebellion. I claim for Chad an awakening of hearts and a turning to the Lord that will transform politics, security, and daily life. Let the altar of the high places be replaced by altars of prayer and righteousness.

Lord God, cause true leadership to arise—interim authorities and future presidents who will govern with transparency, justice, and a heart for every region of the land. Displace corruption and tribal favoritism; replace deceit with accountability and policies that deliver water, food, and hope. Give the nation wisdom to care for displaced families and the influx of refugees, and let Christlike compassion flow from both church and state. Raise up Christian broadcasters, storytellers, and radio ministries in Chadian Arabic that carry the gospel into camps and towns, softening hearts and stirring faith among Muslims and animists alike.

Father, send laborers and Bible storytellers into the isolated villages; empower believers from Muslim backgrounds with boldness and love to reach their own people. Strengthen grassroots discipleship so that converts are rooted, taught, and sent. Break the power of violence and banditry that prey on the vulnerable; protect the young and feed the hungry. Let education flourish as a place where truth and skill meet, and the literacy rate rises as people learn skills for life and ministry.

I prophesy stability and revival over Chad: that famine's grip will loosen, that peace will be established in contested regions, and that the Church will become a conveyor belt of mercy and mission across the nation. Let Chad walk into her destiny as a kingdom-blessed people marked by justice, peace, and a multiplying witness for Jesus.

In Jesus' name, Amen.

41

CHILE

"He has showed you, O man, what is good; and what does the LORD require of you, but to do justice, and to love kindness, and to walk humbly with your God?"
— Micah 6:8 WEB

Righteous Judge and Lover of Justice, I present Chile before You—her cities, her youth, and her traditions. I declare that Chile will be known for doing justice, loving kindness, and walking humbly with its God. Break the tides of moral drift, materialism and despair; restore the good fruit of the family and social structures that uphold flourishing. Let the Spirit of wisdom and of counsel infuse leaders, pastors, teachers, and parents so that decisions produce dignity for young mothers, protection for children, and restoration for those trapped in addiction or crime.

Lord, bring cultural renewal that balances liberty and holiness. Where liberalization has brought harm, bring sober wisdom; where reform has brought relief, prosper and preserve that good fruit. Raise up local church movements that connect with students, artists, and families—expressions of faith that are culturally resonant and spiritually powerful. Ignite church planting among the least reached pockets, and let the Evangelical witness increase in authenticity and compassion so that many will see Christ lived before they hear His name.

Heal the wounds of young women and men who bear the burden of early pregnancy, poverty, and broken homes. Strengthen social services, create pathways for education and vocation, and expose trafficking and drug networks that prey upon the vulnerable. Empower Chilean Christians to lead in schools, hospitals, and civic life with humility and excellence, offering holistic solutions that reflect the heart of Christ.

I prophesy a Chile where mercy and truth embrace—a nation that models justice and kindness; where churches multiply and families are strengthened; where the gospel wins whole communities and the Kingdom of Christ takes deep root. May Chile's streets and homes echo with the praise of a people restored.

In Jesus' name, Amen.

42

People's Republic of China

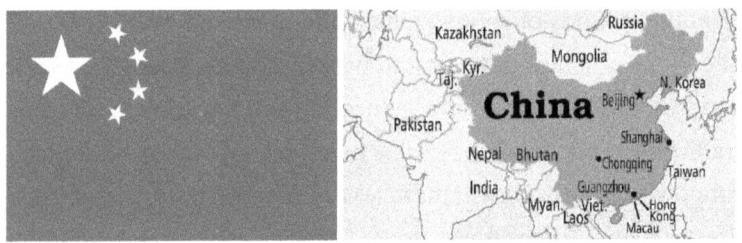

"You are the light of the world. A city set on a hill cannot be hid."
— Matthew 5:14 WEB

Lord Jesus, radiant King and light of every nation, I lift China before Your throne and declare that she shall be a shining city on a hill as churches and believers arise glowing with Your presence. Where darkness of control, oppression, and displacement have overshadowed millions, let the light of Christ penetrate every province. Bring supernatural boldness to the house churches, perseverance to the imprisoned, and divine creativity to gospel workers who reach the migrant poor, the elderly, and those abandoned by systems.

Father, empower Chinese believers with wisdom to love their neighbors in tangible ways: feeding the hungry, caring for the aged, and bringing dignity to those left by rapid urban migration. Multiply discipleship networks that are culturally rooted and spiritually vibrant. Strengthen networks in Henan, Zhejiang, and the regions where revival has been fierce; let those sparks spread to East, Central, South, and the remote high places of Tibet and Xinjiang. Equip the Church to carry the gospel to unreached minorities with humility and sensitivity, breaking down ethnic pride and paternalism.

Lord, protect and grow the Back to Jerusalem vision with humility and sound training. Raise up missionaries ready to cross cultural lines, and grant the Church wisdom to send rather than to dominate. Bless seminary students, underground preachers, and those who print and distribute Scripture. Comfort and strengthen those who suffer in prison and labor camps; let their faith shine and transform guards, officials, and neighbors.

I prophesy a great awakening in China: from city apartments to rural villages, from factories to university campuses—Your light will not be hidden. The Church will be a beacon of healing, truth, and hope; Chinese believers will labor with sacrifice and joy to see nations touched. Let China be counted among those nations whose God is the LORD.

In Jesus' name, Amen.

43

Colombia

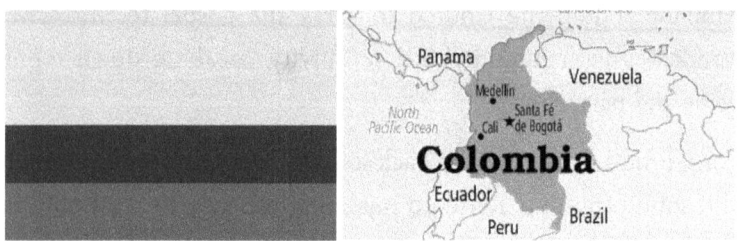

"The Spirit of the Lord GOD is upon me; because the LORD has anointed me to preach good news to the poor; he has sent me to bind up the brokenhearted, to proclaim liberty to the captives, and the opening of the prison to them that are bound."
— Isaiah 61:1 WEB

Compassionate Savior and Prince of Peace, I bring Colombia before Your throne—her cities scarred by violence, her countryside longing for lasting peace, and her streets crowded with the weary and with refugees from Venezuela. I call the anointing of the Spirit to rest upon this land: preach good news into places of hurt, bind up broken hearts, and proclaim true liberty to captives of addiction, crime, and past trauma. Let the Church arise as a healing presence where the wounds of decades find balm.

Lord, grant the justice processes strength and wisdom so that truth and reconciliation bring restorative justice rather than revenge. Protect those who work for victims—pastors, lawyers, counselors—and empower them to bring both accountability and healing. Pour supernatural favor upon churches that reach out to Venezuelan migrants; let Colombian believers be known for generous hospitality, practical care, and gospel proclamation that meets both physical and spiritual need.

I pray for Amerindian tribes who suffer discrimination and spiritual isolation. Send translators, courageous workers, and protective ministries to finish Scripture translations and plant culturally rooted churches. Preserve the identity and dignity of these peoples; prevent exploitation of their lands and stop violence toward them. Raise up disciples within the 15 isolated tribes before their chance for the gospel passes.

Father, let peace settle like a garment over Colombia. Disband the networks of drug cartels and revive communities with education, opportunity, and economic alternatives. Bless leaders who pursue reconciliation and social renewal; let the rule of law be infused with wisdom and compassion. I prophesy a Colombia where the anointing leads to multiplied churches, healed families, and an economy that uplifts the poor—a nation where Your Kingdom comes in power and love.

In Jesus' name, Amen.

44

COMOROS

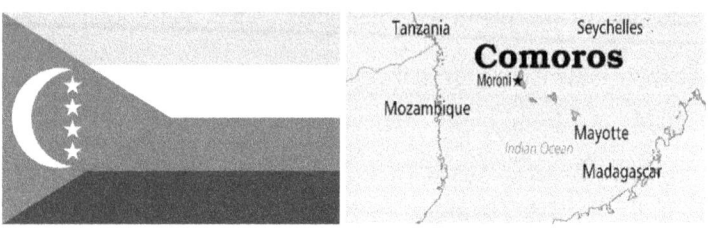

> "Arise, shine; for your light has come, and the glory of Yahweh has risen upon you."
> — Isaiah 60:1 WEB

Lord Most High, I stand before Your throne as an intercessor for the islands of Comoros and I declare with prophetic authority that the darkness that has long covered these shores will not remain. I call forth Your light to break through the strongholds of fear, Islamism, occult oppression, and the spirit influences of witchcraft and curses that have enslaved many. I claim for this small nation the dawning of Your glory so that the people who wander in spiritual night might see a radiant hope and be drawn into the Kingdom. This is a strategic moment—the islands will not be written off; rather, they will arise and shine with testimonies of redemption.

Father, I plead for the spread of the gospel among the 66% who are unevangelized and among the predominantly Muslim communities. Let Your church be incarnational and wise; send gentle, courageous workers who will meet people where they are—in mosques, markets, and villages—bringing the living Christ through acts of service, love, and truth. Break the chains of spiritual deception: expose every lie of occult power and tear down every altar built in secret. Replace fear with the peace of Christ; replace bondage with joy. Raise up local evangelists and discipleship networks that will not merely convert but ground new believers in the Scriptures, prayer, and community, equipping them to withstand opposition.

O Lord of compassion, stir economic and social opportunities so young people are not driven by despair into drugs, sex, or escape. Let vocational training, fair work, and education flourish across Moroni and the outer islands so that hope and futures appear where none were seen. Bless those who bring healthcare, literacy, and counselling; let the literacy rate climb as Your truth is taught and as hearts open. I release a prophetic burden for the islands' leaders: grant them integrity and a desire to protect the vulnerable, to steward resources justly, and to create space where the Church can minister without unnecessary fear.

Holy Spirit, move mightily to create a harvest among families previously closed to the gospel. Let testimonies of freedom multiply until whole communities are transformed. I prophesy that Comoros will become a place where the oppressed find deliverance, where the young are given purpose, and where the light of Christ shines from every shore. Let this generation arise and shine for Your glory. In Jesus' name, Amen.

45

REPUBLIC OF CONGO (ROC)

"Seek the welfare of the city where I have sent you into exile, and pray to Yahweh for it; for in its welfare you will have welfare."
— Jeremiah 29:7 WEB

Sovereign King and Counselor, I lift the Republic of Congo before Your throne and declare that Brazzaville and every province will be under the wise governance of Your Spirit. I speak peace and stability over a nation recovering from the wounds of civil strife and the legacy of political upheaval. I call for a turning of hearts toward the common good—that leaders, civil servants, and citizens will pursue policies of justice, stewardship, and prudence so that the nation's potential is no longer wasted. Let the welfare of the city become the welfare of the people, and let Your blessing flow as leaders choose life and prosperity for all.

Father, grant those in authority godly wisdom to steward the natural resources—oil, timber, and minerals—with righteousness and accountability. Where greed and mismanagement once robbed the people, raise up governors and economic stewards who operate with transparency and integrity. Let laws protect the vulnerable and penalize exploitation; release judges and civic leaders who will rule in fairness. I ask for economic policies that generate jobs, lift families from poverty, and fund education and healthcare so that life expectancy and quality of life rise across the nation.

Lord Jesus, breathe revival into the churches of the Congo so that Christian influence becomes a constructive force for nation-building. Strengthen pastors and mission leaders to train workers and to deploy them to rural and urban centers alike. May the church lead in social services, literacy, and reconciliation ministries, healing old divisions and nurturing national unity. Multiply Gospel initiatives among the small unevangelized pockets, and equip believers to be peacemakers between communities once divided by conflict.

Holy Spirit, uproot the remnants of violence and fear that linger in many hearts. Bring restoration to displaced families and comfort to those who still bear the scars of war. I prophesy a Congo renewed—a nation where justice flows like a river and where the people prosper because leaders and citizens alike seek the common good. May Brazzaville and every town be a place of flourishing under Your reign. In Jesus' name, Amen.

46

DEMOCRATIC REPUBLIC OF CONGO (DRC)

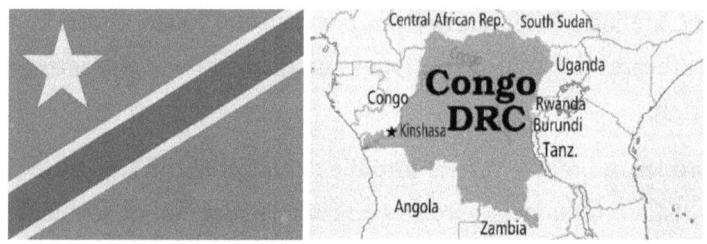

"God is our refuge and strength, a very present help in trouble."
— Psalm 46:1 WEB

Mighty Deliverer and Redeemer, I stand as a watchman over the vast expanse of the Democratic Republic of Congo and I declare that this land will no longer be a theatre of unending sorrow but a stage for Your victory. You are the refuge for the millions who have suffered generations of exploitation, brutality, and war; I call Your saving presence into eastern forests, mining regions, and refugee camps. Let Your strength arise in the churches and in the hearts of ordinary citizens so that they will be emboldened to resist evil, to rescue the exploited, and to proclaim Christ's justice with courage.

Father, rip away the coverings that have allowed foreign plunder and internal greed to pillage the nation's resources. Expose those who profit from suffering; let international networks of manipulation be disrupted and replaced with fair, God-honoring stewardship. Release an awakening of prophetic accountability into the marketplace, the mines, and the halls of power so that transparency and repentance become the new norm. Raise up leaders who will prosecute wrongdoers, protect women and children from sexual violence, and create systems of justice that bring healing rather than more harm.

Lord Jesus, pour supernatural comfort and psychological healing into communities traumatized by rape, cannibalism, and witchcraft influence. Equip the Church with trained counselors and deliverance ministries that bring holistic recovery—body, mind, and soul. Send mission teams to the remote villages with medical care, trauma counselling, Scripture, and sustainable community projects that restore dignity and hope. Empower grassroots discipleship that even children and youth can engage in, so the next generation will rise with faith instead of bitterness.

Holy Spirit, bind the demonic systems that have held sway and break their power now. Let the light of Christ dispel the darkness of occult practices; let testimonies of healing and justice multiply across Kinshasa, Goma, and every province. I prophesy that the DRC will become known not for its tragedies but for its restoration—a nation whose riches serve its people, whose churches lead in compassion, and whose sons and daughters walk in liberty. In Jesus' name, Amen.

47

COOK ISLANDS

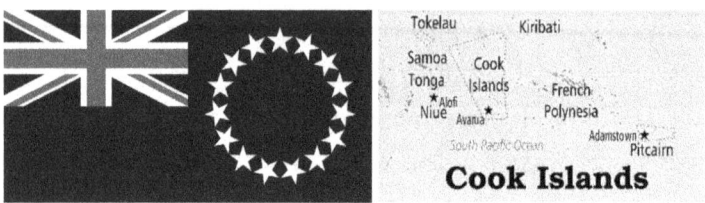

"Behold, I will do a new thing; now it will spring up; will you not know it? I will even make a way in the wilderness, and rivers in the desert."
— Isaiah 43:19 WEB

Lord of new beginnings, I raise the Cook Islands before Your throne and declare that the long Christian legacy upon these isles will be renewed with fresh fire. Though a strong heritage of faith exists, I prophesy a reversal of nominalism and spiritual drift. The churches that once shaped islands and families will recover their prophetic voice, and a new generation will arise who know You personally rather than merely inherit a faith. Let the old pillars be rekindled, and let rivers of living water flow where spiritual dryness has crept in.

Heavenly Father, send revival to Avarua and across each island, awakening hearts to the beauty and demands of gospel living. Stir pastors and lay leaders to preach humility, holiness, and radical love—not cultural Christianity that tolerates compromise, but a living faith that transforms homes, schools, and governance. Raise up worshippers, evangelists, and youth movements that reclaim the islands for Christ; let Sunday gatherings overflow and community outreach become the norm, drawing back those who have drifted into nominalism, secularism, or other faith groups.

Lord Jesus, heal the cultural wounds that make faith merely traditional for many. Bring discipleship models that honour Cook Island cultures while rooting believers deeply in Scripture. Empower the churches with creative approaches to engage young people—through art, music, service, and mentorship—so that faith becomes attractive, credible, and contagious. May the best of mainline denominations be refreshed and renewed with the Spirit's power, and may faith be expressed with both reverence and relevance.

Holy Spirit, open doors for unity among churches so that the gospel is presented clearly and unashamedly across every village and harbor. I prophesy that the Cook Islands will experience a spiritual spring: new converts, multiplied small groups, and a reclaimed commitment to Christ that influences not only private devotion but public life. Let this chain of islands again be known as a place founded upon Your truth and living under Your reign.

In Jesus' name, Amen.

48

COSTA RICA

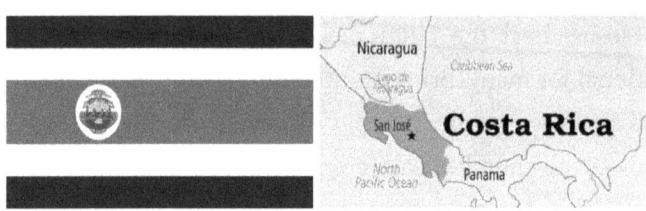

"All the saints were to come to the unity of the faith and of the knowledge of the Son of God, unto a full grown man, unto the measure of the stature of the fullness of Christ."
— Ephesians 4:13 WEB

Sovereign Lord and Master Teacher, I stand in the gap for Costa Rica and declare that Your Church in San José and across every valley and mountain will rise into spiritual maturity. I prophesy an end to shallow converts and a birth of disciples who know Jesus intimately and walk in the fullness of His character. Let the equipping gifts You appoint for the building up of the body be released now—pastors, teachers, and leaders empowered to train saints for works of service so that your people stop being easily moved by every wind of doctrine.

Father, pour out provision for pastors who survive on meager incomes; multiply workers, resources, and sustainable support models so shepherds are freed to shepherd and to disciple deeply. Let seminaries, Bible schools, and informal training hubs multiply and become fertile fields of spiritual formation. I ask that faithful mentorship networks arise where leaders intentionally invest in new believers and help them stand when difficulties come, preventing the pattern of falling away or church-shopping that has weakened witness. Raise up teams that design contextually strong discipleship systems—small groups, apprenticeship, and family discipleship—that fit Costa Rica's culture and reality.

Lord Jesus, move across the nation among the 93.9% who name Christ and among the 14.8% Evangelicals to shift from mere confession to conviction. Where numerics exist without depth, send revival that births conviction, obedience, and perseverance. Bless the one Least Reached people group with sensitive, humble outreach that honours their language and culture. Let literacy and Bible engagement thrive—families reading Scripture together, young leaders understanding doctrine and worshipping in spirit and truth. May the Church's influence extend into schools, workplaces, and government through lives transformed by love, holiness, and wisdom.

Holy Spirit, release a fresh anointing for mission and mercy across Costa Rica: sustained discipleship, healthy church structures, pastors who are nourished, and saints who mature into Christlike leaders. I prophesy a movement where converts are counted as disciples and where entire communities are shaped by the fruit of steadfast faith. Let the Kingdom come in Costa Rica until Christ is formed in every believer. In Jesus' name, Amen.

49

CÔTE D'IVOIRE

"That they all may be one; even as you, Father, are in me, and I in you, that they also may be one in us; that the world may believe that you sent me."
— John 17:21 WEB

Sovereign God of reconciliation and true unity, I lift Côte d'Ivoire before Your throne and decree that the walls of division built by ethnicity, region, and religion will fall. From Yamoussoukro to Abidjan, I call heaven's unifying power to bind hearts together across north and south, Muslim and Christian, animist and urban neighbor. Let the oneness You prayed for take flesh in the national life so that political ambition no longer rides upon ethnic fault lines and so that the children of this land learn to live as one people under Your justice.

Father, raise leaders who will govern with integrity and who value national unity above partisan gain. Replace corruption with accountability, and selfish ambition with servant leadership that invests in education, healthcare, and long-term development. Let national policies be crafted with the welfare of every region in view, especially the young—nearly forty-two percent under 15—so that generations are not stolen by neglect. Turn influential voices in media, business, and churches toward peacemaking and structural justice, and clothe officials with humility and wisdom.

Lord Jesus, strengthen the Church across denominations: Catholic, Methodist, Evangelical and the many newer independent fellowships. Increase theological depth so that believers truly know Scripture and do not substitute prosperity for discipleship. Multiply Bible training institutes and effective pastoral formation so that congregations are led by grounded teachers who disciple rather than merely gather crowds. Bless the steady growth of evangelicals while maturing their faith; let truth and love shape how the gospel is preached and practiced among all people groups, including the 24% still unevangelized.

Holy Spirit, send a wave of relational reconciliation—truth-telling balanced with forgiveness, restorative justice instead of revenge. I prophesy Côte d'Ivoire as a nation where differences are honored but unity prevails, where churches are catalysts of peace, and where the world sees in this diverse country the beautiful oneness of Christ's body. Let the Kingdom rule and justice roll like a river through every town and village.

In Jesus' name, Amen.

50

CROATIA

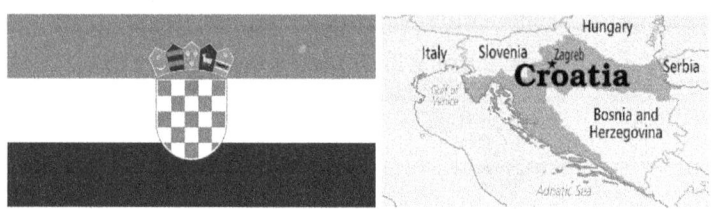

"He has given to us the ministry of reconciliation, that God was in Christ reconciling the world to himself, not imputing their trespasses unto them; and he has committed to us the word of reconciliation."
— 2 Corinthians 5:18–19 WEB

Lord Jesus, Prince of Peace and Healer of Memory, I come before You on behalf of Croatia and declare that the ministry of reconciliation will sweep this land. Where old wounds between Croat, Serb, and Bosnian have left bitterness, trauma, and suspicion, I call Your reconciling presence to mend what hate has torn. Let churches be at the forefront of truth-and-grace work, bringing real restoration to hearts and communities so that historical animosities lose their power and new generations grow up reconciled in You.

Heavenly Father, empower the Catholic Church and other faithful leaders who are already working toward healing—bless their initiatives, strengthen their resolve, and give them supernatural effectiveness. Raise up counselors, trauma-care teams, and community restoration projects that address the psychological and emotional scars that linger from conflict. Equip pastors and lay workers with deep pastoral skills so that families and communities can process grief, confess wrongs, and rebuild trust. Release funds, volunteers, and partnerships to sustain long-term reconciliation efforts rather than short-lived responses.

Lord, set loose a fresh humility among political, civic, and religious leaders to model repentance, peacemaking, and shared civic responsibility. Where nationalism and hurt memories have hardened hearts, soften them with the spirit of Christ who stooped to reconcile enemies. Let educational curricula and public discourse support truth-telling accompanied by restorative action, preventing the next generation from inheriting an antagonistic worldview. Bless church-driven social initiatives that provide jobs, youth mentorship, and platforms for cross-ethnic cooperation.

Holy Spirit, breathe a renewal across Zagreb and every town—a renewal that is not merely sentimental but deep and lasting. I prophesy Croatia becoming a place where reconciliation is normal, where churches lead in healing, and where the world witnesses the transforming power of Christ's forgiveness. Heal the land, restore relationships, and let the Kingdom reign in every heart.

In Jesus' name, Amen.

51

CUBA

"It is for freedom that Christ has set us free. Stand firm therefore, and do not submit again to a yoke of slavery."
— Galatians 5:1 WEB

Sovereign Redeemer and Liberator, I lift the island nation of Cuba before Your throne and proclaim liberty for Havana and every barrio. You have called the Cuban people into a freedom that is more than political; it is spiritual and social restoration. I take hold of that liberty now—loosening the chains of poverty, oppressive systems, and the spiritual strongholds that have fed black markets, crime, and the despair that drives people to flee. Release a righteous freedom that brings dignity, hope, and economic renewal.

Father, bless the Cuban diaspora with the gospel's influence—let those who left become missionaries of reconciliation and channels of wisdom, resources, and prayer back to their homeland. Soften hearts in the leadership to pursue prudent reforms that allow entrepreneurship, protect basic freedoms, and care for the vulnerable rather than imprison them. Where hundreds of thousands have been wrongfully detained and millions displaced, move in justice and mercy; bring restorative policies, family reunification, and renewed social structures that sustain the elderly and youth alike.

Lord Jesus, empower churches and house fellowships amidst persecution to be lights of compassion—training centers that provide literacy, vocational skills, and counselling for those damaged by imprisonment or consequence of economic collapse. Raise a generation of Cuban leaders in business, medicine, and the arts who are formed by the gospel and return to serve their nation's renewal. Break industries built on sexual exploitation, drugs, and exploitation; replace them with enterprises that honor human dignity and provide honest livelihoods.

Holy Spirit, stir forgiveness and repentance where required, and let abundant grace produce tangible transformation. I prophesy a Cuba rebuilt in righteousness: families restored, industries purified, pastors emboldened, and a nation walking in that true freedom which Christ purchased. May the Cuban Church be a primary agent of the island's healing and revival.

In Jesus' name, Amen.

52

Curaçao

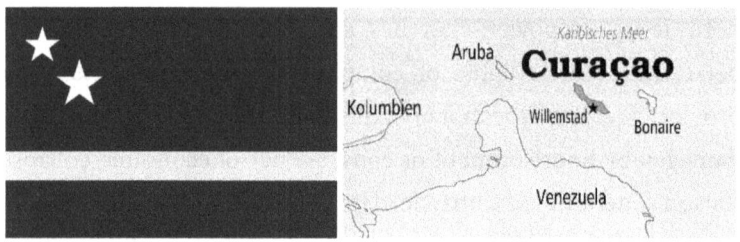

"All Scripture is inspired by God and is profitable for teaching, for reproof, for correction, for instruction which is in righteousness; that the man of God may be complete, furnished completely unto every good work."
— 2 Timothy 3:16–17 WEB

Lord of Wisdom and Word, I lift Curaçao and declare that Your Word will take deep root across Willemstad and every neighborhood where Papiamento is spoken. Bless the Papiamento Scriptures and may they pierce hearts, instruct households, and equip saints for every good work. I prophesy an upsurge in biblical literacy that transforms devotion into discipleship, church attendance into life transformation, and cultural faith into a living, doctrinally sound witness.

Father, multiply the distribution and use of the Papiamento Bible and Christian literature—print more copies, digitize resources, and fund literacy programmes that help the majority-language speakers read and digest God's Word. Bless the Christian bookstore and local publishers with expanded inventories, and send educational ministries to partner with churches and schools so that Bible teaching becomes the backbone of spiritual formation in homes. Raise up translators and theologians who can produce accessible devotional and discipleship material in Papiamento for all ages.

Lord Jesus, empower pastors and lay leaders to teach with clarity and relevance, moving people from shallow cultural Christianity into a deeper knowledge of doctrine and practice. Encourage the mainline churches and evangelical fellowships to cooperate in theological education and to create apprenticeships that sustain small congregations. Address the two least-reached people groups among the sixteen on the islands through culturally respectful outreach that honors their languages and ways, while offering the transforming Word.

Holy Spirit, breathe a renewed hunger for Scripture across Curaçao so that believers are equipped to live righteously and to serve their communities. I prophesy a flourishing of literacy, multiplied ministries in Papiamento, and a Church so well taught by Scripture that it stands as a beacon for the Caribbean—full of sound doctrine, vibrant discipleship, and works of love.

In Jesus' name, Amen.

53

CYPRUS

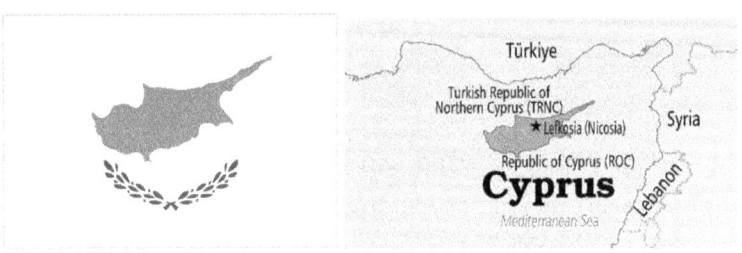

"Blessed are the peacemakers, for they shall be called sons of God."
— Matthew 5:9 WEB

Sovereign Lord of Heaven and Earth, I stand before You as an intercessor for Cyprus and I declare in faith that the voices of peacemakers will arise across Lefkosia (Nicosia) and every divided town. I prophecy that the blessing reserved for those who make peace will be poured out upon those who choose reconciliation over revenge, dialogue over suspicion, and unity over division. Let the spiritual identity of peacemaker be stamped upon pastors, civic leaders, teachers, and ordinary families so that they act with courage and wisdom to dismantle fifty years of estrangement.

Father, bring a deep work of repentance and forgiveness across both Greek and Turkish communities. Where memory hardens into grievance, break the chains and heal old wounds; where external meddling has fanned animosities, confound those agendas and give Cypriots sovereignty of heart to pursue their shared future. Make the crossing of the dividing line more than a bureaucratic act—let it be a pathway to hospitality, joint projects, interfaith friendship, and cooperative commerce. Pour out humility on the few who insist on intransigence so public sentiment for reunification may translate into concrete, courageous steps.

Lord Jesus, renew the spiritual life of the island: strengthen churches to model reconciliation and equip them to teach neighbor-love across cultural lines. Raise up a generation of young leaders fluent in both Greek and Turkish, who will serve as bridge-builders in schools, local councils, and marketplaces. Let the 12% who remain unevangelized hear with clarity and encounter a Christian witness marked by peace, compassion, and Christlike truth. Provide resources for cross-community ministries—trauma care, joint youth programs, and shared economic development—that heal hearts while meeting needs.

Holy Spirit, breathe a fresh wind of unity over Cyprus: unite families formerly divided, convert suspicion to trust, and replace foreign manipulation with local stewardship. May the island be known as a place where the peacemaking blessing is lived out publicly, where reconciliation transforms society, and where God's rule brings real and lasting unity. Let Cyprus move into a unified future by Your grace and power.

In Jesus' name, Amen.

54

CZECHIA

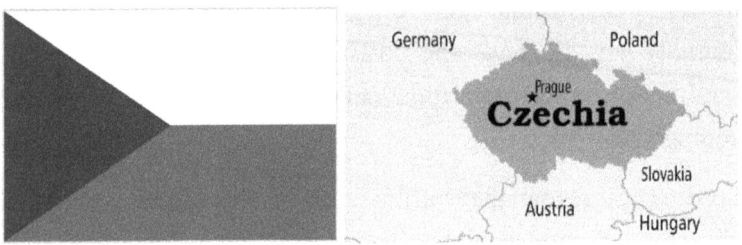

"Do not be conformed to this world, but be transformed by the renewing of your mind, that you may prove what is that good and acceptable and perfect will of God."
— Romans 12:2 WEB

Lord of truth and renewal, I lift Czechia before Your throne and declare a fresh transformation across Prague and every town where secularism and spiritual confusion have settled in. I call Your renewing power to invade minds and cultures so that people once trapped in relativism and superstition are awakened to the life of Christ. Let intellectual hunger be met by living encounters with Jesus; let the lie that truth is unknowable be broken by the clarity of the gospel. I prophesy a mental and spiritual revival that restores mental health, hope, and moral courage in families and communities.

Father, break the grip of hopelessness, substance abuse, and despair that rise in a land of high non-religious identification. Pour out resources for holistic healing—mental health ministries integrated with Christian care, addiction recovery programs rooted in discipleship, and community centers that offer dignity, skill training, and safe places for youth. Bless church plants and mission initiatives that reach Russian-speaking immigrants and East/Southeast Asian communities with culturally sensitive gospel tools. Let new believers be grounded, not superficial, so converts will become stable disciples, teachers, and neighbors.

Lord Jesus, equip a new generation of Czech pastors, counselors, and lay-workers with theological depth and practical compassion. Raise up small groups and mentoring networks that disciple believers into maturity and resilience, preventing the pattern of falling away under pressure. Reintroduce the goodness of Christian marriage, family values, and community responsibility without coercion but with winsome excellence, so that society sees the fruit of a life transformed.

Holy Spirit, return wonder and curiosity to Czech hearts: kindle a hunger to test and prove God's will rather than drift with cultural currents. I prophesy that Czechia will become a place where renewed minds prove the goodness of God's ways, where the non-religious encounter living truth, and where healing replaces despair—a nation shaped by the revealed will of God.

In Jesus' name, Amen.

55

Denmark

> "But sanctify the Lord God in your hearts, and always be ready to give an answer to every man that asks you a reason concerning the hope that is in you, with meekness and fear."
> — 1 Peter 3:15 WEB

Lord God of compassion and reason, I lift Denmark before Your throne and declare that the Danes will rediscover the living Christ who first shaped their laws, art, and community life. I call for a sanctifying work in hearts across Copenhagen and every town so that Christ becomes not merely a cultural memory but the enthroned Lord of private life and public testimony. Release a new hunger for truth and a respectful boldness among believers to give a gentle and winsome defense of their hope.

Father, empower churches to be places of deep charity and sound teaching that meet Danes in their search for meaning. Equip pastors and lay leaders with apologetic gifts and cultural sensitivity so they can engage agnostic and spiritual seekers with clarity and compassion. Multiply outreach that addresses loneliness, mental health, and generational drift—ministries that restore community in neighborhoods, universities, and workplaces. Let public servants and artists who shaped Danish life regain courage to speak about faith in ways that invite exploration rather than provoke reaction.

Lord Jesus, pour out a fresh holiness that is attractive, not legalistic; grant believers humility and winsome courage to answer questions about faith and to demonstrate it in deeds. Bless media, literature, and pedagogy that present the gospel with excellence and truth. Where tradition is empty ritual, replace it with Spirit-filled living; where agnosticism is a shield, let curiosity be reborn. Give Danish churches a renewed capacity for discipleship so converts are nurtured into stability and service.

Holy Spirit, stir an awakening that balances reason and devotion. I prophesy a Denmark where the faithful are ready to answer, where seekers find Christ through both word and deed, and where the nation rediscovers the spiritual roots that formed its life. Let the Kingdom come in Denmark—quietly, wisely, and powerfully.

In Jesus' name, Amen.

56

DJIBOUTI

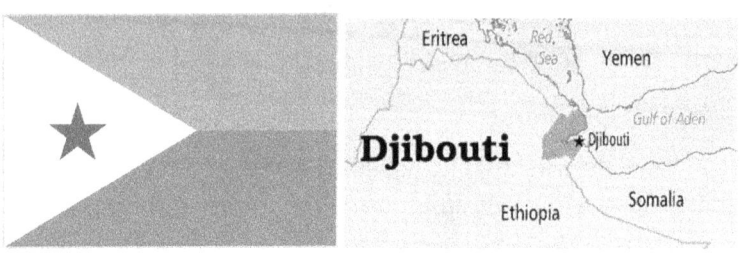

"Defend the poor and fatherless; do justice to the afflicted and needy. Deliver the poor and needy; rid them out of the hand of the wicked."
— Psalm 82:3–4 WEB

Mighty Defender and Just Judge, I present Djibouti before Your throne and declare that the vulnerable in this nation will find a divine protector. Rise up, O God, as the defender of the poor, the trafficked, and the exploited along the coasts and in urban camps. Where famine, unemployment, human trafficking, and drug abuse press hard upon people, let Your justice move swiftly to rescue, protect, and restore. Let the tiny Christian witness in Djibouti be emboldened and multiplied to care for the afflicted with practical mercy and gospel clarity.

Father, bless the Western presence that provides some stability, but let true security come from the Lord. Prevent Islamist domination from strangling freedoms and opportunities; guard the public square so that the few Christians present can serve without fear and so humanitarian work may continue. Empower churches and NGOs with wisdom to identify and dismantle trafficking networks, to rehabilitate survivors, and to offer vocational training that replaces exploitation with dignity and stable livelihoods.

Lord Jesus, send prayerful workers who understand Somali and Afar cultures, who will plant contextual fellowships and compassionate ministries that anchor the community. Raise local leaders from within Djibouti's people who will not be mere expatriate initiatives but indigenous movements, multiplying disciples among families and neighborhoods. Let literacy and health programs accompany evangelism so that hearts open through care and lives are transformed by truth and service.

Holy Spirit, release a mantle of protection over children and young people—nearly 30% under fifteen—and let their futures be guarded by effective education and employment pathways. I prophesy that Djibouti will become a place where injustice is confronted, the needy are delivered, and the light of Christ brings structural and spiritual renewal. Let Your justice roll and Your compassion heal this land.

In Jesus' name, Amen.

57

DOMINICA

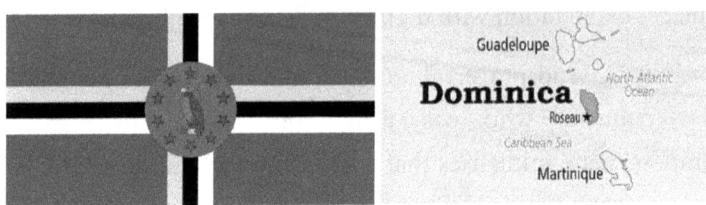

"For the grace of God has appeared, bringing salvation to all men, instructing us to deny ungodliness and worldly lusts, and to live soberly, righteously, and godly in this present world; waiting for the blessed hope and appearing of the glory of our great God and Savior Jesus Christ."
— Titus 2:11–13 WEB

Glorious Savior and Hope of Nations, I lift Dominica and Roseau before Your throne and declare that the islands will know the reality of grace that saves and transforms. Where Catholic practice has become nominal and many have drifted from heartfelt devotion, release a fresh visitation of grace that awakens true repentance, deep discipleship, and persistent holiness. Let faith be more than habit; let it be vibrant, life-shaping, and attractive to the next generation who now stand on the brink of indifference.

Father, empower the churches to teach sound doctrine and to model godly living with practical influence. Bless Catholic leaders, evangelical pastors, and community elders with renewed zeal to disciple families, to nurture youth, and to preach the full counsel of God's Word. Equip ministries to speak into the Creole-speaking heart of the nation so that the gospel lands culturally and linguistically—not as foreign dogma but as familiar truth that heals and reforms daily life.

Lord Jesus, stir the young in Dominican schools and villages with a hunger for holiness and truthful living. Provide programmes of mentorship, vocational training, and community service that root faith in responsibility and love. Replace nominal religion with sacrificial service: let believers be the first to feed the hungry, to care for the elderly, and to mentor the next generation. Multiply small groups and family discipleship networks that hold believers accountable and nurture spiritual growth.

Holy Spirit, bring a revival of grace across the islands: grace that instructs, reforms, and beautifies life. I prophesy Dominica to become a place where nominalism is corrected, where the reality of salvation is lived, and where the blessed hope is joyfully awaited—a people marked by sober righteousness and radiant faith.

In Jesus' name, Amen.

58

DOMINICAN REPUBLIC

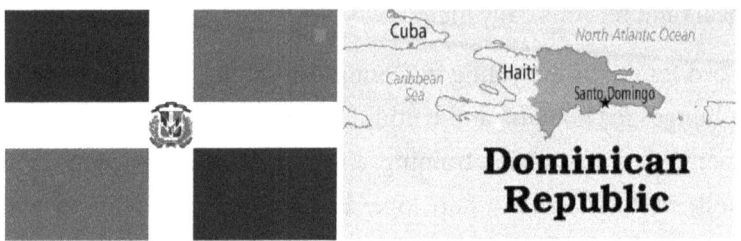

"But let justice roll down as waters, and righteousness as an ever-flowing stream."
— Amos 5:24 WEB

Sovereign Judge and Redeemer, I stand before Your throne as a watchman for the Dominican Republic and I declare that Your river of justice and Your ever-flowing stream of righteousness will flood Santo Domingo and every province. I speak prophetically against the long history of exploitation that has bled this land—colonial theft, forced labor, and systems that enriched a few at the expense of the many—and I release heaven's correcting current to wash clean injustice at every level. Let the course of history be altered by Your compassionate, penetrating righteousness that demands restoration for those who have been dispossessed.

Father, raise up leaders who will hear Your voice and govern with integrity. Where economic structures continue to favor elites and foreign interests, bring reformers who steward resources for the flourishing of families and communities. Bring legal reforms and enforcement that secure land rights, protect the poor, and create economic channels that empower local enterprise rather than exploit it. Stir the Dominican Church to become a prophetic conscience in society—calling rulers to account, advocating for economic justice, and partnering in sustainable development so the long legacy of pain will yield to a future of dignity and hope.

Lord Jesus, work powerfully in the hearts of the young—nearly twenty-eight percent under fifteen—that they would not inherit bitterness but a longing to build a just yet generous society. Empower churches to provide robust discipleship, vocational training, and mentorship that lead to stable homes and honest livelihoods. Let Christian ministries be models of ethical business and community transformation: cooperative agriculture, microfinance, and education programs that break cycles of exploitation. Mobilize the diaspora to be channels of blessing and wise investment that uplift families rather than drain them.

Holy Spirit, pour out Your conviction and mercy together—let truth and compassion walk hand in hand. I prophesy a Dominican Republic that refuses to be defined by centuries of injustice but is remade by rivers of righteousness: land reform, honest markets, restored families, and churches leading in both mercy and justice. Let the Kingdom come in deeds as well as words, bringing healing and hope to every neighborhood.

In Jesus' name, Amen.

59

Ecuador

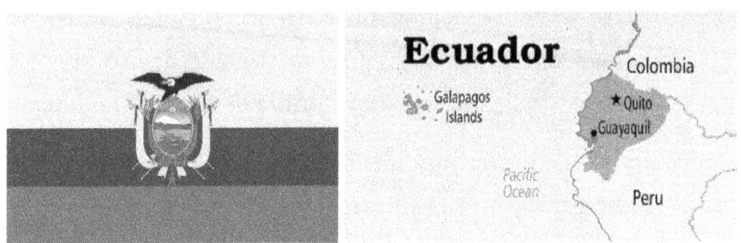

"Your word is a lamp to my feet, and a light to my path."
— Psalm 119:105 WEB

Lord of the harvest and Keeper of every promise, I lift Ecuador before Your throne and declare that Your Word will continue to be the lamp lighting Quito's hills, the Amazon's villages, and the highland paths of the Quichua. I prophesy that Scripture, faithfully taught and beautifully translated, will guide hearts, transform cultures, and sustain movements of discipleship that began in humble tents and radio studios. Let the history of miraculous gospel fruit among the Quichua and Waorani be multiplied until every people group in Ecuador knows and walks in the light of Your truth.

Father, strengthen the institutions that have sown into the Quichua revival and the broader outreach—mission teams, local pastors,

Bible schools, and broadcasting ministries—so that discipleship follows conversion and churches mature into communities of endurance. Bless HCJB's legacy and similar media by gifting new channels, translators, and technicians who can carry the Word into remote valleys and city slums. Protect and provide for the one Least Reached people group; give culturally wise workers who both translate Scripture and embody the gospel in ways that honor language and tradition.

Lord Jesus, deepen the roots of faith among those who came to Christ in the past century. Where converts were numerous but training was thin, raise up shepherds to disciple families into stable, reproducing faith. Multiply Bible teachers, mentors, and small group leaders who will model godly marriage, parenting, and community life. Let churches be centers of healing and practical care: clinics, schools, and livelihoods that demonstrate that the Word not only teaches but transforms daily living.

Holy Spirit, shine as lamp and path across Ecuador—from the city to the jungle and the coast. I prophesy renewed missions vision, sustained discipleship, and a rise of Ecuadorian workers sent out with humility to the nations. May every step taken by Your people be guided by Scripture's clear light until the whole land walks in the fullness of Christ's Kingdom.

In Jesus' name, Amen.

60

EGYPT

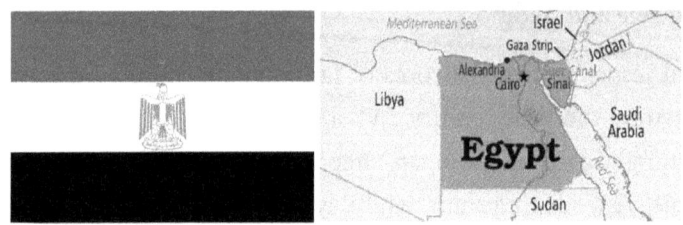

"Blessed be Egypt my people, and Assyria the work of my hands, and Israel my inheritance."
— Isaiah 19:25 WEB

Ancient God, whose name was known in temples and hermitages long before modern borders, I present Egypt before Your throne and declare that the time of blessing is appointed for her land and people. You who have woven Egypt into redemptive history will not abandon her—though many pressures, political shifts, and persecution have made faithful living costly, I call heaven's favor to the Coptic communion, to house churches, and to every believer who bears the risk of discipleship. Let the Church's historic roots be honored and its present witness expanded so that Egyptians discover anew their sacred inheritance as recipients of Your blessing.

Father, grant wisdom to rulers so that governance restrains evil without crushing conscience. Where extremist currents threaten freedoms, provide just restraint; where authorities marginalize Christian contribution, bring recognition for the Church's ancient role and future service. Protect congregations from violence and legal harassment, and use the global diaspora and local leaders to advocate for rightful presence and participation. Raise up public servants and reformers who will strengthen civil life, protect minorities, and support the flourishing of families, churches, and scholarship.

Lord Jesus, heal centuries of estrangement and empower the Egyptian Church to be a fortress of compassion—feeding the hungry, caring for widows, and restoring the traumatized. Equip pastors and elders with courage to teach deep theology and with creativity to reach urban Muslims, youth, and those searching for meaning. Let Christian institutions—hospitals, schools, and ministries—serve visibly and winsomely so society experiences the gospel in practical mercy and in truth.

Holy Spirit, fall on Egypt as You did on nations before: awaken the faithful, embolden the fearful, and multiply testimonies that draw many to Christ. I prophesy a new season where Egypt is both blessed and a blessing—where ancient faith and renewed witness together push back darkness and reveal the light of the gospel across the Nile and beyond.

In Jesus' name, Amen.

61

EL SALVADOR

"And it shall be afterward, that I will pour out my Spirit on all flesh; and your sons and your daughters shall prophesy..."
— Joel 2:28 WEB

Mighty God of restoration, I stand in the breach for El Salvador and declare the outpouring of Your Spirit across San Salvador and every barrio afflicted by gangs, poverty, and broken families. I call heaven's wind to sweep through neighborhoods where maras have cruelly claimed youth and hope, and I prophesy that Your Spirit will kindle prophetic courage in pastors, parents, and young leaders so they will speak truth, demonstrate mercy, and lead recovery movements for a traumatized generation. Let this nation experience not only reduced violence but spiritual renewal that endures.

Father, penetrate the structures that feed gang recruitment—poverty, lack of education, and absent hope—with comprehensive solutions rooted in both policy and the gospel. Move leaders to enact social programs that create jobs, fund vocational training, and offer safe spaces for youth. Empower churches to become centers of refuge and rehabilitation: offering counseling for trauma, programs that teach skills, and discipleship that replaces gang identity with Kingdom identity. Multiply initiatives that connect remittances and diaspora goodwill with locally sustainable enterprises.

Lord Jesus, raise missionary pastors and prophetic community organizers who will reclaim streets with the Gospel's presence. Where corruption has eroded trust, bring transparent leadership and community-led accountability. Strengthen families and mentors to invest in boys and girls at risk, and beautify neighborhoods with restorative community projects that inspire civic pride and hope. Let churches be known for practical mercy: feeding programs, after-school care, and reconciliation circles that heal wounds and prevent cycles of vengeance.

Holy Spirit, pour out revival that leads to transformed lives, communities, and institutions. I prophesy that El Salvador will move from terror to testimony—gangs will lose territory as churches and honest commerce take root; families will be healed, and a generation will rise prophetic and peaceful. Let Your Kingdom come and Your will be done in El Salvador as in heaven.

In Jesus' name, Amen.

62

Equatorial Guinea

"For everyone to whom much was given, from him much will be required."
— Luke 12:48 WEB

Righteous King and Judge, I lift Equatorial Guinea before Your throne and declare an accounting of stewardship over every barrel of oil, every transaction, and every policy. This nation that has been flooded with resources for the few will now be visited by an economy redeemed to serve the many. I call heaven's conviction upon corrupt systems and release wisdom and repentance upon leaders so the wealth extracted from beneath the soil will be stewarded with equity, foresight, and compassion rather than squandered in private gain.

Father, anoint reformers and impartial institutions that will establish transparent governance and ensure that oil profits fund schools, hospitals, and sustainable infrastructure. Protect whistleblowers and empower civic servants committed to the common good. Bring multinational companies into partnership with local communities rather than exploitation; let contracts and practices be rewritten so local people benefit in jobs, training, and long-term wealth that remains after oil runs low. Raise up local entrepreneurs and vocational programs that diversify the economy and prepare the nation for a post-oil future.

Lord Jesus, stir the expatriate church and visiting believers to engage sacrificially—not as temporary visitors but as partners in education, healthcare, and church planting that bless the nation long-term. Equip local churches to teach stewardship and kingdom economics so Christians model transparency and service in business and government. Let the Church be a prophetic conscience, calling rulers to justice and showing practical models of equitable business.

Holy Spirit, convict hearts where greed has blinded them and inspire a national ethic of responsibility. I prophesy a future for Equatorial Guinea where abundant resources become abundant blessings: children fed, elders cared for, education flourishing, and the Church leading in moral renewal. May those entrusted with much be found faithful, and may the nation's true wealth be measured by the flourishing of its people.

In Jesus' name, Amen.

63

ERITREA

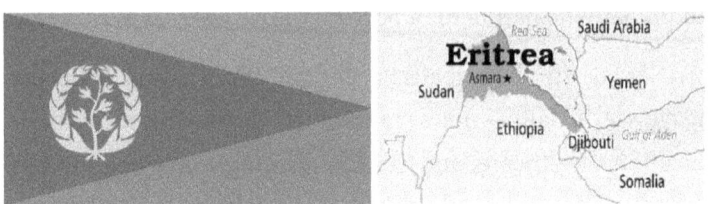

"Blessed are those who are persecuted for righteousness' sake, for theirs is the kingdom of heaven."
— Matthew 5:10 WEB

Sovereign Lord and Defender of the oppressed, I stand in the gap for Eritrea and declare prophetically that Your blessing rests upon Your people even amid suffering. I call heaven's favor and the reality of Your kingdom to infiltrate Asmara and every village where fear, compulsory conscription, and restriction of conscience have pressed down the people. Though many feel hunted and constrained, I lift up Your promise that those who endure for righteousness will be counted among Your kingdom— so I release endurance, courage, and an ever-deepening hope into the hearts of believers across the nation.

Father, loosen the grip of systems that crush human dignity: bring an end to exploitative mandatory service that steals youth and fractures families, and open pathways for the diaspora's remittances to be used for rebuilding communities, not just survival. Raise up courageous advocates of human rights within and outside government who will press for restorative reform. I ask that doors be opened for the 29% who remain unevangelized to hear the gospel through compassionate witness—medical care, literacy programs, sustainable agriculture, and trauma counselling—so the Church's witness becomes both word and generous deed.

Lord Jesus, grant the underground churches spiritual boldness and wise strategies. Where registration laws have silenced fellowship, give ingenuity in discipleship, safety in worship, and multiplied leaders trained in theology and pastoral care. Strengthen those Christian traditions allowed public space—Orthodox, Catholic and recognized communities—to be beacons of mercy, modeling how the gospel cares for the poor, feeds the hungry, treats the sick, and heals the wounded in spirit. Let reconciliation ministries move between religious communities so mutual respect and peace grow.

Holy Spirit, release revival that translates into restored freedoms and practical relief: rains for drought, supply lines for food, renewed workforce participation, and compassionate governance that values life over control. I prophesy a future where Eritreans experience both justice and joy, where religious freedom increases, families are reunited, and the kingdom's reality breaks the power of persecution. Your church in Eritrea will stand as living proof that even in trial the Lord's dominion advances.

In Jesus' name, Amen.

64

Estonia

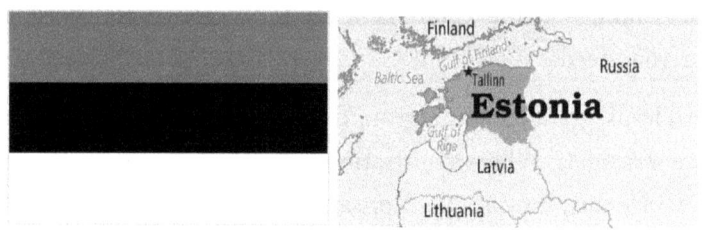

"For I know the thoughts that I think toward you, says Yahweh, thoughts of peace, and not of evil, to give you an expected end."
— Jeremiah 29:11 WEB

Lord of purpose and peaceful designs, I present Estonia before Your throne and declare that the people of Tallinn and every Estonian town will awaken to the hope You have planned for them. In a land where secularism has become a wide horizon and material appetite increasingly defines success, breathe into the nation a renewed sense that life is held in Your wise hands, that You think toward this people with a future of peace, and that their deepest longings will find fulfillment in You. I release prophetic hope to those who feel spiritually adrift.

Father, send a fresh wave of spiritual seekers who will trade skepticism for genuine encounter. Equip churches to meet minds and hearts with winsome truth, to disciple in depth, and to present Christian convictions with intellectual integrity and cultural sensitivity. Raise up ministries that reach Russian-speaking communities and immigrants with translated resources and warm hospitality, and bless campus ministries that stand as islands of light in universities where secular thought dominates. Let public leaders model a moral seriousness that resists greed even as the economy grows.

Lord Jesus, transform the crisis of values into an opportunity for Gospel formation: teach Estonians the beauty of self-giving, the dignity of community, and the glad discipline of sacrificial living. Multiply mentor-apprentice relationships so new believers become grounded in Scripture and practice. Strengthen family life and local congregations so they become centers of compassion for the vulnerable and engines of societal renewal. Raise up a generation that chooses stewardship over consumption and service over self.

Holy Spirit, move across Estonia to restore minds, revive hearts, and anchor a people in Your peaceful purpose. I prophesy a nation that discovers the expected end You have arranged—peace that steadies, meaning that satisfies, and communities that bear witness to the God who knows and loves them. Let Estonia become an example of thoughtful faith lived with courage and grace.

In Jesus' name, Amen.

65

Eswatini

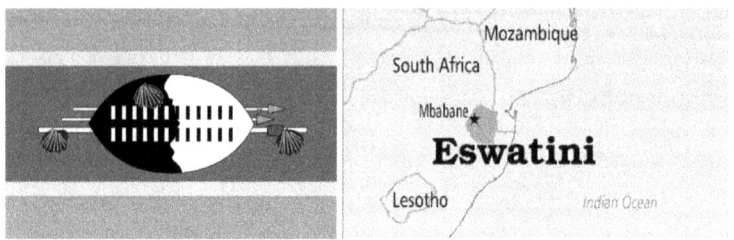

"When the righteous are in authority, the people rejoice:
but when the wicked bear rule, the people mourn."
— Proverbs 29:2 WEB

King of Kings and Lord of rulers, I lift Eswatini before Your throne and declare that Your righteousness will be the measure of leadership on which the nation's welfare depends. I call Godly sight into the monarchy and those who advise the king: may they see their office as sacred stewardship rather than mere privilege. Replace extravagance with servant-hearted rule; where lavishness has separated palace from people, let humility and a sense of responsibility for the poor and unemployed take root, so that governance produces rejoicing rather than mourning among the nation.

Father, stir the king's heart to govern for the common good—to use influence to alleviate the deep poverty and low life expectancy, to provide honest employment opportunities, to open political space for civic participation, and to prioritize health and education for the many who suffer. Soften the armor of intransigence that resists accountability and let conviction guide policies that elevate human dignity. Bless those close to leadership with godly counsel, integrity, and a vision for equitable development that includes training, micro-enterprise, and investment in rural livelihoods.

Lord Jesus, raise grassroots Christian movements across Mbabane and rural chiefdoms that are compassionate, disciplined, and strategically organized to meet needs where the state cannot. Let local churches be hubs of social care—feeding programs, job training, clinics and youth mentorship—so that the Church models kingdom alternatives to dependency. Empower evangelists and discipleship trainers to equip the faithful to be citizens of influence: entrepreneurs, teachers, community leaders who transform villages with gospel-saturated service.

Holy Spirit, breathe renewal through Eswatini: break cycles of apathy, push back against systems that marginalize, and ignite a culture of servant leadership. I prophesy a monarchy and a people reshaped by righteousness—where the needy find relief, the unemployed find dignity, and the nation rejoices under leaders who rule in godly fear. Let the Kingdom come, changing both palace and plain.

In Jesus' name, Amen.

66

ETHIOPIA

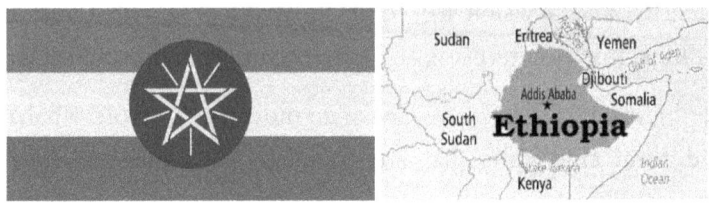

> "Envoys shall come out of Egypt; Ethiopia shall hasten to stretch out her hands unto God."
> — Psalm 68:31 WEB

Ancient God, Giver of nations and Sustainer of peoples, I present Ethiopia before Your throne and prophesy a great turning toward You across Addis Ababa, the highlands, the lowlands, and every tribe. In a nation scarred by conflict, ethnic division, and humanitarian crisis, release a swift movement of reconciliation and reaching—envoys of mercy and missionaries of peace—so that long-standing wounds are met with healing presence and countless hands are lifted to You in faith. Let the posture of seeking God become widespread and urgent across every people group.

Father, bring an end to the cycles of violence that have ravaged regions and displaced millions. Soften hard hearts, dismantle militaristic pride, and bind the spirits of revenge. Raise statesmen and local leaders who pursue equitable power-sharing and inclusion, policies that value each ethnic group, and economic measures that close the gap between the few wealthy and the many impoverished. Provide for the immediate humanitarian needs of 20 million affected people—food, medical care, shelter—and grant long-term plans for agriculture, education, and infrastructure that restore stability.

Lord Jesus, breathe fresh vitality into the Ethiopian Orthodox Church and the many evangelical movements alike—renew ancient liturgy with living faith, and strengthen newer churches with sound doctrine and sacrificial service. Equip clergy, catechists, and lay-leaders with pastoral skill to address trauma, with theological depth to resist syncretism, and with bold compassion to lead reconciliation projects. Multiply Bible translation, literacy, and discipleship among the 15% unevangelized so that the gospel becomes indigenous and widely embraced.

Holy Spirit, stir a national repentance that leads to justice, mercy, and unity; let restoration follow redemption. I prophesy Ethiopia rising from its wounds as a testimony to God's reconciling power—where rival ethnicities build one people under Your lordship, where children learn without fear, and where the Church catalyzes lasting peace and flourishing for all. Let Your kingdom come in Ethiopia as in heaven.

In Jesus' name, Amen.

67

FALKLAND ISLANDS

"The LORD will give strength to his people; the LORD will bless his people with peace."
— Psalm 29:11 WEB

Sovereign Lord of the nations, I rise as a watchman and declare over the Falkland Islands that your blessing of peace and strength will come upon Stanley and every settlement. I prophesy that the weary memory of conflict and the heavy question of sovereignty will not define the islanders' future; instead, Your peace will govern negotiations, relationships, and hearts. I plead that Your peace—not political pressure or coercion—be the atmosphere that frames every discussion between the islands, the United Kingdom, and Argentina. Let Your strength uphold islanders as they seek wise autonomy and fair, dignified agreements.

Father, grant wisdom and humility to the diplomats and leaders engaged in these complex conversations. Where pride and old strategic interests have hardened positions, pour out a spirit of compromise that treasures people over politics. Let agreements be crafted with fairness and anchored in respect for the Islanders' desire for self-governance, while also providing stability for the wider region. Soften foreign agendas that press for advantage; replace bargaining with genuine listening, and supply creative, durable solutions that secure both dignity and economic flourishing for islanders and neighboring nations.

Lord Jesus, breathe reconciliation into communities still bearing scars from past conflict. Raise up Christian leaders and intercessors who will model peacemaking, who will offer hospitality and mutual understanding, and who will minister to veterans and families affected by the 1982 struggle. Equip congregations to be agents of healing—hosting forums, joint memorials, and shared civic projects that bind wounds in practical ways. Let educational and cultural exchanges deepen relationships so that next generations inherit trust rather than suspicion.

Holy Spirit, sustain the small population with tangible provision: healthy public services, robust local economy, and secure fisheries and shipping industries. Multiply initiatives that strengthen civic life—local leadership training, transparent governance, and stewardship of natural resources. I prophesy the Falkland Islands becoming an example of wise self-governance and faithful peacemaking—an island people whose strength is rooted in the Lord and whose peace blesses surrounding waters and nations.

In Jesus' name, Amen.

68

FAROE ISLANDS

"Create in me a clean heart, O God, and renew a right spirit within me."
— Psalm 51:10 WEB

Holy and merciful Father, I stand in the breach for the Faroe Islands and declare that You are beginning a deep, cleansing work among the people of Tórshavn, the isles, and every valley. I prophesy inner renewal that moves beyond nominal Christianity into a living, humble devotion—hearts humbled, cleansed, and filled anew with the Spirit. Let the upsurge of prayer houses and Pietist movements not be a momentary breeze but the birthing of a sustained, God-centered revival that transforms households, schools, and civic life.

Lord Jesus, stir the Lutheran tradition and the evangelical bodies alike to united spiritual hunger. Where form has replaced fire, replace ritual with repentance; where comfort has dulled conviction, rekindle sacrificial love. Empower pastors and prayer leaders to teach deeply, to disciple thoroughly, and to model holiness that is attractive and winsome. Let the 35 prayer houses and thousands of affiliates be hotbeds of intercession, outreach, and service that overflow into community compassion: care for the elderly, outreach to youth, and practical support for struggling families.

Father, send the Spirit to birth evangelistic zeal that is both culturally sensitive and truth-filled. Equip congregations to reach the nominal and the unchurched with both relational warmth and doctrinal clarity. Raise up musicians, teachers, and entrepreneurs who will express the gospel in ways that resonate with Faroese identity—work that honors language, sea-faring heritage, and family life. Let Sunday gatherings be renewed with depth and joy so that consistent worship and discipleship become the norm again.

Holy Spirit, bind the forces of complacency and call every church to a holy unrest for God's glory. I prophesy the Faroes becoming truly Christian in spirit and practice: a people marked by confession, repentance, rigorous discipleship, and a contagious devotion that draws islanders back into faithful living. Let this revival be measured not by numbers alone but by transformed hearts, lasting holiness, and communities bearing the fruit of righteousness.

In Jesus' name, Amen.

69

FEDERATED STATES OF MICRONESIA

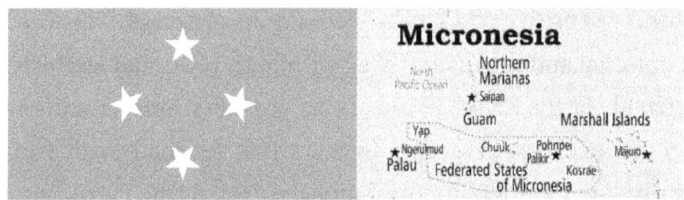

> "Be filled with the Spirit; speaking to yourselves in psalms and hymns and spiritual songs, singing and making melody in your heart to the Lord."
> — Ephesians 5:18–19 WEB

Lord of islands and oceans, I lift the Federated States of Micronesia before Your throne and declare that the islands will be filled with the Spirit—songs of praise rising from Yap to Pohnpei, Chuuk to Kosrae—transforming cultural practices, narcotic cravings, and consumerist drift into heartfelt worship and holy purpose. I prophesy a spiritual reformation across Palikir and every atoll in which the power and love of Jesus displace magical practices, the seductive pull of communal narcotics, and the empty promises of Western materialism. Let the islands sing again with truth that gives life.

Father, give cultural wisdom to the Church in Micronesia so that the gospel engages—not destroys—honored customs, distinguishing what honors God from what enslaves. Guide pastors and elders to present Jesus as the one who satisfies deeper than sakau or superstition, replacing communal narcotic rituals with wholesome communal practices—festivals of praise, vocational initiatives, and community service that honor island identity while offering freedom. Strengthen Christian families to model sobriety and godly lifestyle so young people see a viable, joyful alternative to migration and dependence.

Lord Jesus, confront the influence of competing faith movements with gentleness and clarity. Where Mormon missionaries and others bring competing narratives, grant Micronesian believers discernment and robust theological roots to hold fast to the gospel. Raise a generation of indigenous leaders—evangelists, teachers, and entrepreneurs—who will harness US aid and external partnerships for Kingdom-building rather than consumer dependency. Provide training in stewardship so aid becomes a bridge to sustainable local enterprise rather than an invitation to idolatry of comfort.

Holy Spirit, ignite a movement where the islands become centers of worship, service, and holiness—where spiritual songs replace escapist rituals and where Jesus-centered community draws many back to healthy living. I prophesy Micronesia as a shining example of gospel-rooted culture: communities strong in identity, free from enslavement, and radiant with the joy and power of Christ.

In Jesus' name, Amen.

70

Fiji

> "He has made of one blood every nation of men to dwell on all the face of the earth."
> — Acts 17:26 WEB

Sovereign Creator and Healer of Nations, I stand as an intercessor for Fiji and declare that the Lord who fashioned all peoples will bring justice, reconciliation, and flourishing to Suva, the villages, and every village line between native Fijians and Indo-Fijians. I call heaven's reconciling power to dismantle long-held suspicions and to build equitable systems where both communities can thrive. Let the legacy of colonial division and the wounds of coups be swept away by a new ethic of mutual respect and shared prosperity under Your rule.

Father, grant wisdom to political leaders to craft policies honoring native cultural rights while protecting equal opportunity for all ethnic groups. Soften hard hearts shaped by historical grievances and strengthen laws that ensure fair land use, education access, and participatory governance. Raise honest leaders committed to fair treatment, not ethnic favoritism; replace grievance politics with constructive, Crops-to-Skills programs that lift households economically and socially. Let vocational training, agricultural support, and microenterprise create pathways where every family can prosper.

Lord Jesus, empower churches to be key agents of reconciliation. Equip pastors and Christian NGOs to design community programs that bring together youth across ethnic lines—sports, arts, job training, and joint service projects that form friendships and build trust. Multiply cross-cultural church plants that intentionally include both communities, teaching shared values of forgiveness, stewardship, and neighbor-love. Provide trauma counseling where past coups left deep psychological scars so that individuals can forgive and rebuild.

Holy Spirit, breathe unity where division once ruled: bless marriages across ethnicities, bless businesses that employ inclusively, and bless public education that honors cultural identity while teaching civic unity. I prophesy a Fiji where difference becomes a source of strength, where native Fijians flourish in their land and Indo-Fijians find fairness and dignity, and where the gospel leads both toward a shared, blessed future. Let the Kingdom come and peace reign across the islands.

In Jesus' name, Amen.

71

Finland

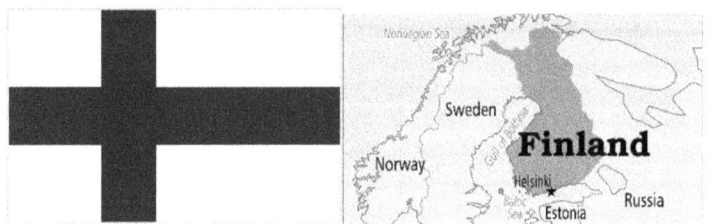

"May the God of hope fill you with all joy and peace in believing, that you may abound in hope by the power of the Holy Spirit."
— Romans 15:13 WEB

God of hope and light, I present Finland before Your throne and declare an awakening of hope across Helsinki, Lapland, and every Finnish town. Let the God of hope fill hearts with joy and peace that spring from believing—so that the sharp rationalism and secularism that have cooled the nation's religious life will encounter a renewing work of the Spirit. I prophesy a fresh hunger for God that combines intellectual rigor with spiritual vulnerability so Finns will not merely admire the Church's social work but will personally meet and follow Jesus.

Father, grant Finnish churches and leaders a renewed vision: reformation within established bodies and the birth of new, creative expressions of faith that fit the modern Finnish mind. Encourage deep theological reflection that engages science, art, and public life, and bless new ministries that present the gospel in winsome, credible ways. Raise contemplative and missional communities that integrate reason with the reality of encounter—places where questions are welcomed and faith is formed through thoughtful discipleship, service, and spiritual formation.

Lord Jesus, release a movement of small groups, campus ministries, and family discipleship that rebuilds consistent worship habits — not out of obligation but from transformed hearts. Provide resources for Saami and Swedish-speaking minorities, and bless ministries that reach the unreached 2% and those who identify as non-religious with humility and excellence. Strengthen Finnish Christians to be articulate witnesses who can present the faith with both depth and tenderness, connecting tradition and contemporary life.

Holy Spirit, pour out joy and peace into Finnish souls so that hope becomes contagious across neighborhoods and workplace cafes. I prophesy Finland to experience a reformation and awakening that honors reason and restores wonder—a nation where thoughtful faith leads to public renewal, robust discipleship, and a younger generation seeking the Lord. May the Kingdom advance in this northern land by a power that renews both mind and heart.

In Jesus' name, Amen.

72

FRANCE

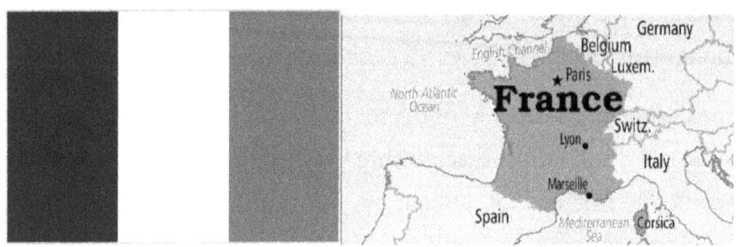

"For he satisfies the longing soul, and the hungry soul he fills with good."
— Psalm 107:9 WEB

Sovereign God of mercy and wisdom, I come before You as a bold intercessor for France and I declare that the deep existential hunger in French hearts will meet its true and lasting satisfaction in You. I lift Paris and every city, town and village where people feel the tremor of uncertainty — aging populations, economic strain, and a searching youth — and I prophesy that the Lord will supply not merely temporary relief but deep spiritual nourishment that changes whole lives. Let the vacuum left by declining ideologies be filled with the living presence of Christ, the only One who finally satisfies.

Father, strike at the roots of economic injustice and systemic indecision that produce the Yellow Vest anger and the weariness of so many workers and middle-class families. Give rulers and economists prophetic wisdom to design reforms that protect the vulnerable, reward honest labor, and create new opportunities for the young. Release creative public policies that balance innovation and tradition, open pathways for immigrants to contribute and be embraced, and restore confidence in the Republic's ability to care for its citizens. Let public discourse be shaped by truth, compassion, and solutions rather than merely anxiety.

Lord Jesus, raise a people-focused Church that can speak into the spiritual hunger of the postmodern mind with both intellectual honesty and compassionate presence. Equip a generation of French believers to be patient witnesses—friends, coworkers, teachers, and neighbors who embody hope rather than peddle ideology. Multiply contextual evangelism that honors French culture and language while proclaiming the gospel clearly; bless campus ministries to meet students who long for meaning; empower small groups that disciple deeply so converts do not drift when trials come.

Holy Spirit, break the walls of suspicion toward organized faith and replace them with credible encounters—healing in families, restored relationships, and communities where the gospel proves itself in deed and word. I prophesy that France will see pockets of awakening where spiritual hunger meets the Bread of Life; that cities and regions will rediscover a hope beyond mere economic respite; and that the Kingdom's rule will increasingly shape public life, art, and policy. Restore the French heart with a lasting joy only You can give. In Jesus' name, Amen.

73

FRENCH GUIANA

"Learn to do good; seek justice, relieve the oppressed; judge for the fatherless, plead for the widow."
— Isaiah 1:17 WEB

Merciful Judge and Defender of the helpless, I lift French Guiana before Your throne and declare that this land will be known for justice, mercy, and protection. I prophesy a turning in Cayenne and throughout the coastal and interior communities where young people face unemployment and families are stretched thin. Let leaders and churches rise together to confront trafficking, environmental harm, and the moral corrosion of media influence. Replace restlessness with purposeful opportunity and healing, and let justice be the norm for the vulnerable rather than the exception.

Father, raise a network of ministries, civic leaders, and business entrepreneurs who will tackle illegal mining, human trafficking, and the environmental ruin that often goes hand in hand with exploitation. Open the eyes of officials to the practical needs of single-parent homes and the many children affected by social fragmentation. Provide vocational training, job creation schemes, and small-business grants to channel youthful energy into lawful productivity. Encourage shady industries to be uprooted and replaced by sustainable enterprises that care for both people and creation.

Lord Jesus, empower the Church to reach the 1–2% unevangelized and the many nominal folk with incarnational love. Multiply Bible engagement and culturally resonant discipleship in Guianese French Creole and indigenous languages so the Word not only informs but transforms families. Bless translation work, local theological training, and youth outreach that addresses pornography's harm and restores moral frameworks through mentorship and wholesome community life.

Holy Spirit, drive revival that combines prophetic justice with abundant mercy: rescue the trafficked, restore the environment, and renew hearts so that French Guiana becomes a place of flourishing. I prophesy churches that lead social renewal, young people who find dignity in honest work, and communities healed from exploitation. Let Your Kingdom come and Your righteousness reign in every valley and shoreline.

In Jesus' name, Amen.

74

FRENCH POLYNESIA

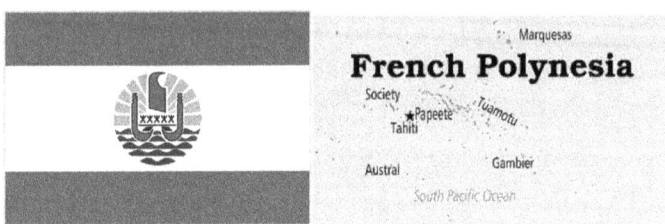

"I will put my Spirit in you, and you will live, and I will place you upon your own land; and you will know that I am Yahweh."
— Ezekiel 37:14 WEB

Almighty God, Breath of life and Restorer of nations, I stand in faith for French Polynesia and declare that Your Spirit will breathe new life into hearts that have grown nominal and lukewarm. From Papeete to remote atolls, I prophesy a spiritual revolution where superficial religion gives way to living faith; where syncretism and occultic entanglements are loosened and genuine devotion to Christ is established in homes, schools, and churches. Let the islands know the reality of God's presence in ways that transform identity and culture.

Father, cause the gospel to address the spiritual void left by nominalism and foreign sects. Empower faithful pastors and lay leaders to preach repentance, teach sound doctrine, and model holiness in culturally sensitive ways that honor Tahitian heritage while calling people to wholehearted worship. Strengthen family discipleship so children are catechized and parents are equipped to nurture spiritual life. Provide resources for Bible translation, theological training, and revival conferences that awaken dormant faith with humility and zeal.

Lord Jesus, displace occult practices and syncretistic religion with testimonies of deliverance, healing, and transformed lives. Let the Spirit convict and convert leaders of influence—traditional chiefs, educators, and cultural figures—so that Christian convictions are expressed authentically across island life. Multiply prayer movements and house churches that sustain believers when larger institutions are weak; let the presence of God become tangible in marketplaces, schools, and seaside villages, drawing many into repentance.

Holy Spirit, pour out a revival that is both deep and lasting: a reformation of the heart, a sweeping of falsehood, and a flowering of genuine worship across the archipelago. I prophesy that French Polynesia will rise as a people who truly live under Yahweh's rule—free from spiritual bondage, renewed in faith, and grounded in the fullness of Christ. Let Your sovereign presence reclaim every island.

In Jesus' name, Amen.

75

Gabon

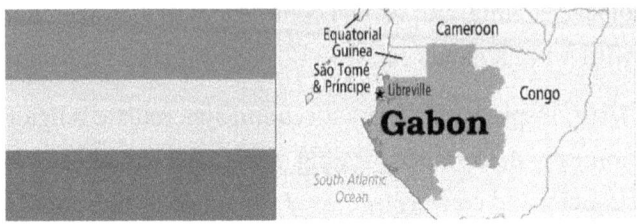

"For we do not wrestle against flesh and blood, but against principalities, against powers, against the rulers of the darkness of this world..."
— Ephesians 6:12 WEB

Mighty Warrior and Conqueror of darkness, I stand in the spiritual gap for Gabon and declare that the occult powers that have subtly shaped cultural and institutional life will lose their grip. I lift Libreville and every town where charms, hallucinogen rituals, and ancestral practices hold sway and prophesy a breaking of those strongholds. Where public officials and security forces have engaged in secret rites, I call the light of Christ to expose darkness and the authority of heaven to bring repentance and deliverance.

Father, strengthen Christians who refuse to participate in witchcraft-related practices despite the cost to career and education. Provide them with visible protection, opportunities for influence, and faithful networks that promote integrity in professional life. Raise prophetic voices that confront the spiritual abuse underpinning corruption and injustice, and bless judicial and civil reforms that penalize exploitation rather than reward occult alliances. Let academic institutions and civic conversations embrace transparency and the rule of law over secret allegiances.

Lord Jesus, pour out healing over communities deceived by spiritist practices; show the power of the gospel through testimonies of freedom from addiction and occult bondage. Equip churches with training in deliverance ministries, pastoral counseling, and practical social services that offer alternatives to witchcraft: clinics, youth programs, schooling, and mentorship. Increase biblical literacy so the Word becomes the authority guiding daily life and not the whisper of ancestral fear.

Holy Spirit, ignite a movement of courageous faith that uproots darkness and plants righteousness—churches that stand faithful, leaders who repent, and citizens who choose truth. I prophesy Gabon emerging as a nation where Christ's light dispels superstition, where ethical leadership is rewarded, and where the Kingdom advances over every altar of fear. Let the people walk free in the liberty of Christ.

In Jesus' name, Amen.

76

THE GAMBIA

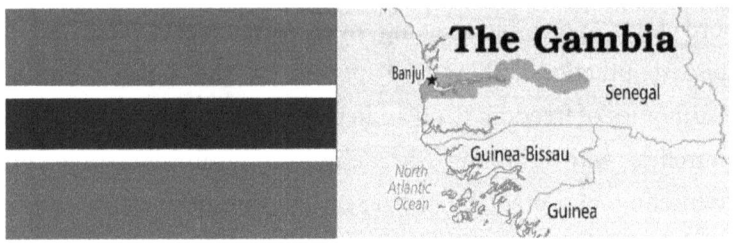

"How then will they call on him in whom they have not believed? and how will they believe in him of whom they have not heard?"
— Romans 10:14 WEB

Lord of the harvest and Lover of the lost, I lift The Gambia before Your throne and declare that the rivers of gospel opportunity will surge upriver into inland villages where many have not yet heard. I prophesy that the friendly relations between Muslims and Christians will be a platform for compassionate witness—Gambian believers stepping out with culturally sensitive love to bring the message of Christ to those who remain unevangelized. Let peace continue, and let it be the soil in which the gospel springs and grows.

Father, provide creative and sustainable support for pastors serving in remote inland regions who now struggle financially. Raise up churches and mission partnerships within The Gambia that prioritize training, micro-finance for leaders, and community projects that relieve poverty and open hearts. Multiply local evangelists who speak native languages, who respect Muslim neighbors, and who weave the gospel into acts of service: wells, clinics, schools, and literacy programmes that demonstrate Christ's love in practical ways.

Lord Jesus, bless the coastal churches in Banjul as sending hubs rather than islands of comfort. Ignite a vision among coastal congregations to invest sacrificially in inland outreach, releasing volunteers, resources, and prayer teams. Empower youth movements to cross cultural lines and build relationships—sports, agriculture, and vocational training that lay foundations for gospel conversations. Strengthen interfaith goodwill so it becomes a bridge rather than a barrier.

Holy Spirit, move mightily across The Gambia to produce both stable relations and dynamic evangelism: inland communities reached, pastors sustained, and Muslims hearing the name of Jesus with clarity and respect. I prophesy a harvest where peace and proclamation walk hand in hand; where Gambians embrace a vision to reach their land; and where the Kingdom expands from river to sea.

In Jesus' name, Amen.

77

GEORGIA

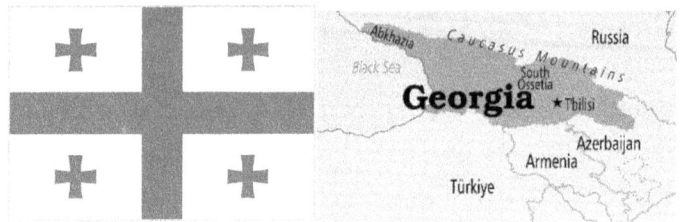

"No weapon that is formed against you will prosper; and every tongue that shall rise up against you in judgment you shall condemn. This is the heritage of Yahweh's servants, and their righteousness is from me, says Yahweh."
— Isaiah 54:17 WEB

Sovereign God, Defender of the weak and Builder of nations, I stand as an intercessor for Georgia and declare that the hand of the Lord will protect her from the schemes and pressures that would steal her peace. I lift T'bilisi and every village under the shadow of foreign influence and regional tension, and I prophesy that attempts to fracture her will be thwarted. Where weapons of division — political manipulation, propaganda, and outside meddling — have been formed, I call forth a hedge of divine protection and the vindicating power of truth that will silence false accusations and bring reconciliation.

Father, breathe wise discernment into Georgia's leaders so that choices about alliances, EU aspirations, and relations with Russia are forged with counsel, humility, and love for the people rather than pride or fear. Turn the fissure between pro-Russian and pro-EU groups into a season of sober dialogue and constructive reform. Raise statesmen who pursue human development as well as economic growth; give them strategies that build schools, healthcare, and job opportunity across regions so the nation's progress is tangible and inclusive.

Lord Jesus, awaken a spiritual hunger that precedes and shapes national progress. Let the Church in Georgia embrace both evangelism and deep discipleship that reach the sixteen least-reached people groups and the 6% still unreached. Send missionaries, equip local seminaries, and raise up culturally fluent evangelists who bridge ethnic and language barriers. May the ancient Christian memory of the land be renewed into a present power of holiness, compassion, and public witness that lifts the nation toward unity and spiritual maturity.

Holy Spirit, heal wounds from past conflict in Abkhazia and South Ossetia with restorative truth and practical compassion — return displaced families, open pathways for dialogue, and bless joint rebuilding projects that knit fabric torn by war. I prophesy Georgia walking into a future where national progress is matched by spiritual depth, where sovereignty is exercised with wisdom, and where the people flourish under God's protective and restorative hand.

In Jesus' name, Amen.

78

GERMANY

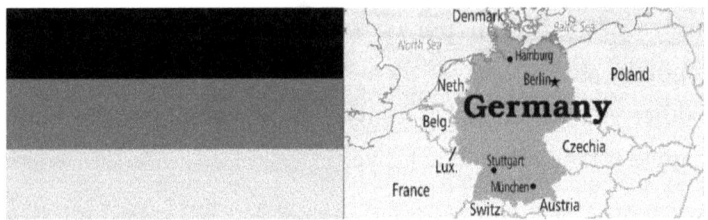

"But you shall receive power when the Holy Spirit has come upon you; and you shall be witnesses to me both in Jerusalem, and in all Judea and Samaria, and to the uttermost parts of the earth."
— Acts 1:8 WEB

Mighty Lord of empowerment and mission, I stand before You as an intercessor for Germany and declare that Your Spirit will bring power to witness in every city from Berlin to the smallest town. I call down the wind of the Holy Spirit to fill churches and hidden prayer rooms so that the German Church, though tested and diminished, will rise with courage and clarity to speak the life-changing truth of Christ. Let this be a new era of witness that embraces immigrants, students, and entire neighborhoods as fields ripe for harvest.

Father, bring an awakening of gospel courage in German leaders of churches and movements — priests, pastors, and lay evangelists who will plant contextual churches among migrant communities and disciple new believers deeply. Give unity across denominational lines where mission demands cooperation and let prayer movements penetrate academic institutions, media hubs, and workplaces. Turn Germany's openness to immigration into a powerful mission field: equip churches to welcome, integrate, and disciple refugees and guest workers so that many become a living testimony to Christ.

Lord Jesus, remove the shackles of intellectual cynicism with encounters that show the love and truth of the gospel. Multiply public theologians, campus ministers, and hospitable families who welcome seekers into study, discussion, and community. Let creative ministries arise in the arts, technology, and business that reflect the gospel with excellence and invite the thoughtful German mind to test the hope offered in Christ.

Holy Spirit, produce a visible change across Germany where hearts are tender and witnesses bold, where refugees find faith communities and churches become hubs of compassionate service and doctrinal faithfulness. I prophesy that Germany's influence in Europe will be leveraged for the Kingdom as believers bring moral courage and spiritual vision into public life. Let the Church be powerfully emboldened to be witnesses to the uttermost parts of the earth.

In Jesus' name, Amen.

79

GHANA

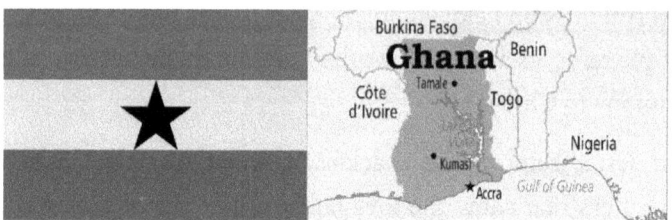

"Trust in Yahweh with all your heart, and lean not on your own understanding. In all your ways acknowledge him, and he will make your paths straight."
— Proverbs 3:5–6 WEB

Sovereign Guide and Source of Wisdom, I come before You for Ghana and declare that the nation's leaders, churches, and families will choose to trust in the Lord rather than in mere human schemes. I lift Accra and every region blessed with youth and diversity, and I call for a divine reorientation toward God's wisdom in governance, education, and community life. Where dependence on human philosophies or ancestral spirits has misled, I declare a fresh turning to the Lord who directs paths and makes crooked ways straight.

Father, bless Ghana's political leaders with humility to seek counsel from You and from wise advisors, not from opportunistic spirits or prideful ambition. Guard leaders from corruption and temptation; raise servants who govern with justice and a heart for the poor. Release policies that retain skilled graduates and incentivize investment at home so that brain drain slows and the nation benefits from its own trained professionals. Empower economic strategies that uplift rural communities, create jobs, and provide sustainable livelihoods for rising youth.

Lord Jesus, deepen the theological maturity of Ghana's fast-growing church landscape. Multiply sound training institutions and mentoring networks so that rapid church growth yields grounded doctrine and ethical practice. Equip pastors and leaders to confront traditional practices of charms and occultism with compassionate truth and deliverance ministry, freeing many into the liberty of Christ. Give pastors the pastoral depth to shepherd youth and families so that regular worship and discipleship become normative.

Holy Spirit, bring unity amid plurality—ethnic groups, denominations, and the many languages will praise one Lord and work together for the common good. I prophesy Ghana as a beacon of stable democracy and vibrant, mature Christianity: a nation where children learn in safe schools, young people find hope, and the Church leads in both righteousness and compassion. Let Your Kingdom come and Your will be done across this beloved land.

In Jesus' name, Amen.

80

GIBRALTAR

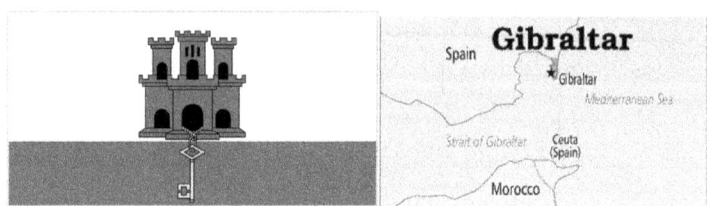

"Go therefore and make disciples of all nations, baptizing them in the name of the Father and of the Son and of the Holy Spirit; teaching them to observe all things whatsoever I have commanded you."
— Matthew 28:19–20 WEB

Lord of the nations and Great Commission King, I lift Gibraltar before Your throne and declare that this strategic rock will be a sending and discipling hub for the region. I call out the evangelistic mantle upon the churches of Gibraltar: let them not merely hold faith inwardly but go forth to reach southern Spain, North Africa, and the many transient visitors who pass through its ports. Release missionary zeal to local congregations so that they not only welcome but equip and send workers into surrounding regions and least-reached people groups.

Father, stir a vision among pastors and lay leaders for outreach that crosses cultural and linguistic barriers: programs in Spanish, Arabic, and other languages that meet the spiritual and practical needs of Moroccans, Jews, Hindus, and the many tourists. Bless training for discipleship that produces mature believers capable of teaching and baptizing new converts. Provide resources and partnerships that strengthen the small evangelical presence and multiply churches that are both culturally sensitive and theologically robust.

Lord Jesus, bless Gibraltar's unique position as a crossroads — let the gospel flow in and out with mercy and truth. Use the ports, businesses, and universities as platforms for witness; let local Christians be hospitable and intentional in mission. Empower youth and emerging leaders to develop outreach projects, mercy ministries, and intercultural initiatives that demonstrate the kingdom in practical ways: English teaching, job training, and community health that open doors for gospel conversations.

Holy Spirit, make Gibraltar a microcosm of Christ's global mission — a place where believers are equipped, sent, and fruitful in neighboring regions. I prophesy a multiplying church presence, strengthened witness to the region, and a people bold in obedience to the Great Commission, leading to many nations hearing and responding to the name of Jesus.

In Jesus' name, Amen.

81

GREECE

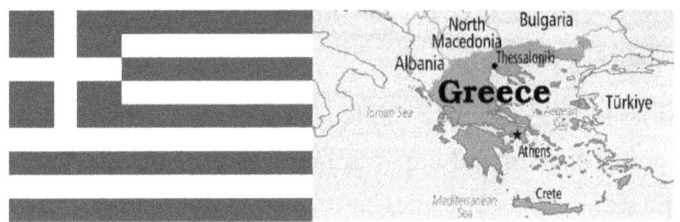

"But you are a chosen generation, a royal priesthood, a holy nation, a people for God's own possession, that you may show forth the virtues of him who has called you out of darkness into his marvelous light."
— 1 Peter 2:9 WEB

Sovereign Lord and Ancient of Days, I lift Greece—Athens, Sparta, islands, and mainland—before Your throne and declare that this cradle of classical thought and the first soil of European evangelism will again rise as a chosen people called to display God's glory. I prophesy that the cultural Christianity of habit will be replaced by living witness: Greeks will move from nominal ritual into authentic relationship, showing forth moral virtue, spiritual clarity, and the radiance of the One who has called them out of darkness.

Father, let the economic and social struggle of the past decades push Greeks to seek answers beyond material fixes and hollow philosophies, drawing many toward the God who offers meaning and hope. Strengthen churches to lead in social restoration—helping families, mentoring youth, and creating job opportunities—so that the pain of austerity and lost opportunities becomes a platform for gospel compassion. Bless recovery ministries, vocational training, and community projects that display the gospel in practical transformation.

Lord Jesus, awaken the evangelical minority with courage and wisdom to proclaim the message afresh—across universities, cafes, and islands. Encourage theological training and cross-cultural outreach so that the message is both rooted in Scripture and presented with cultural sensitivity to Greek identity and history. Multiply small groups and house churches that form disciples who live out priestly witness in neighborhoods and workplaces.

Holy Spirit, resurrect the Macedonian zeal for missions in modern Greece: stir hearts to evangelize with gentleness and conviction, to repent with humility, and to worship with renewed passion. I prophesy a Greece where the Church leads in social healing, where ancient heritage meets present repentance, and where the light of Christ brightens streets and shores — a people renewed and radiant for God's glory.

In Jesus' name, Amen.

82

GREENLAND

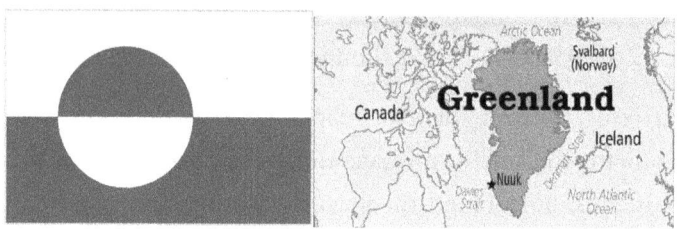

"But those who wait on Yahweh shall renew their strength; they shall mount up with wings like eagles, they shall run and not be weary, they shall walk and not faint."
— Isaiah 40:31 WEB

Sovereign Lord, Ancient of Days and Gentle Healer, I stand as a watchman over Greenland and declare by faith that a renewing wind from Your presence will breathe life into Nuuk and every settlement. I speak strength into hearts battered by modern collisions of culture and tradition; I prophesy that those who have been bowed down by immorality, abuse, alcoholism, mental anguish, and suicidal despair will find fresh stamina by waiting on You. Let waiting on the Lord become a widespread practice—quiet dependence that produces renewed capacity to rise, to run with endurance, and to walk through long nights without fainting.

Father, pour out supernatural resources to strengthen counseling ministries, pastoral care, and deliverance teams already at work among indigenous believers and foreign servants. Multiply the effectiveness of those airstrips and the ministry teams who now reach remote communities; use them to deliver both practical help and the Word that heals. Raise and fund competent counselors, trauma-trained pastors, and community workers who know local language and culture, so that healing is sustainable, not sporadic. Bring programs for addiction recovery, protective measures against sexual abuse, and mental-health initiatives that are culturally wise and spiritually grounded.

Lord Jesus, fan into flame the embers of true worship in the Lutheran churches that dot every settlement; replace nominalism with fervent devotion. Let liturgy and catechesis be gateways to a living relationship, not just ritual. Equip churches to be safe havens of restoration where families gather, children are taught God-honoring values, and wounded souls find restoration. Empower local leaders—elders, youth workers, teachers—to model sobriety, resilience, and Christlike compassion so that community culture shifts away from harm toward holiness.

Holy Spirit, release a sustained revival that brings both immediate rescue and long-term transformation: fewer suicides, fewer addictions, thriving families, and communities that reflect God's renewing power. I prophesy Greenland rising like an eagle—wiser, stronger, and steady—its people renewed by waiting on Yahweh, walking in hope, and living out the freedom only You can give.

In Jesus' name, Amen.

83

GRENADA

"But my God shall supply all your need according to his riches in glory in Christ Jesus."
— Philippians 4:19 WEB

Faithful Provider and Sustainer, I lift Grenada before Your throne and declare that the God who owns the cattle on a thousand hills will meet every pressing need of St. George's and every ravaged valley. I call heaven's provision to the island—resources to rebuild resilient housing, innovative support for agriculture, and sustainable models for tourism that do not re-entangle the people in crippling debt. Let divine provision come with wisdom so that what is rebuilt will withstand the increasing fury of storms and bring lasting flourishing rather than fleeting recovery.

Father, release debt relief, creative finance, and generous partnerships that ease the external burdens which bind the nation.

Soften the hearts of lending institutions and international partners to restructure obligations in ways that free Grenada for long-term regeneration. Inspire local entrepreneurs and civic leaders to adopt sustainable agricultural practices, climate-smart tourism, and disaster-resistant infrastructure. Provide training and micro-capital to families and cooperatives so households can create steady income streams that do not depend on fragile systems.

Lord Jesus, visit the churches and Christian leaders across the island with courage and strategic compassion so that faith becomes the engine of recovery. Let congregations lead in practical relief—community rebuilding teams, counseling for trauma from repeated disasters, and programs that teach resilience and stewardship. Raise a generation of leaders in business and government shaped by gospel values—prudence, service, and sacrificial love—so that national planning protects the vulnerable and invests in the future.

Holy Spirit, bring also a deep spiritual correction: help Grenadians place hope in You above all, even as they pursue material recovery. Rekindle trust in God's sufficiency so that finances are handled with wisdom and not panic. I prophesy Grenada stepping from crisis into sustainable renewal—homes rebuilt, economies diversified, and a people secure in the providence of their God. Let the island become a model of resilience blessed by heaven.

In Jesus' name, Amen.

84

GUADELOUPE

"And we know that all things work together for good to them that love God, to them who are the called according to his purpose."
— Romans 8:28 WEB

Sovereign Redeemer and Healer of Nations, I lift Guadeloupe before Your throne and declare that the complexities of identity, colonial wounds, and economic frustration will be woven by Your hand into a tapestry of healing and purpose. I speak hope into Basse-Terre and Pointe-à-Pitre: the righteous longings for dignity, autonomy, and fair treatment will not be wasted, but God will use them to press Guadeloupe toward greater justice, cultural integrity, and flourishing. Let every grievance that leads to unrest become a catalyst for constructive reform and communal renewal.

Father, grant leaders in both Guadeloupe and France uncommon wisdom and humility to craft policies that heal historical disadvantages rather than deepen them. Soften pride on both sides, and open channels for long-term investment in wages, healthcare, education, and local industry that honors Guadeloupean identity. Replace top-down decrees with participatory planning that includes local voices, especially youth suffering unemployment and cultural alienation. Provide jobs and vocational pathways that restore dignity and reduce the sense of being second-class citizens.

Lord Jesus, empower the Church and Christian leaders to be mediators of reconciliation and practical reform. Let congregations champion social justice—supporting single parents, combating human trafficking tied to illegal gold mining, and offering programs that protect youth from exploitation and moral corruption. Multiply literacy and cultural programs that celebrate Guianese identity while teaching economic skills and civic responsibility. Use Christian media and community workshops to rebuild trust and to facilitate dialogue that prevents violent polarization.

Holy Spirit, bring a genuine awakening that fuses justice with mercy across Guadeloupe: wounds acknowledged, systems restructured, and communities flourishing. I prophesy this island moving from resentment toward restorative action—where history is honored but not weaponized, where identity is celebrated and opportunity grows, and where God's purpose brings beauty from complexity. Let Your Kingdom come in Guadeloupe.

In Jesus' name, Amen.

85

GUAM

"Endeavoring to keep the unity of the Spirit in the bond of peace."
— Ephesians 4:3 WEB

Prince of Peace and Unifier, I stand as an intercessor for Guam and declare that the Spirit's unity will come to Palau's neighbors and to Guam's multicultural congregations alike—binding diverse tongues and traditions into one joyful, peaceful witness. I prophesy that the many denominations, immigrant communities, and tribal cultures will find a strong, humble unity that does not erase identity but deepens mission: a Church that is beautifully diverse yet profoundly united in Christ's love and purpose, equipped to reach both villages and modern towns with the gospel.

Father, grant leaders across Chamorro, Filipino, Korean, Chinese, and Micronesian communities a shepherd's heart that values cooperation over competition. Replace fragmentation with networks of mutual support—shared training for pastors, joint outreach to isolated villages, and cooperative ministries that address animistic influences with wisdom and compassion. Provide funding and practical support for the evangelistic challenge among remote Micronesian groups, equipping local believers to serve effectively while honoring their cultural heritage.

Lord Jesus, bless Guam's churches with ministries that address generational needs: youth discipleship in a modernizing context, family counseling that counters the pull of harmful traditions, and worship that includes multiple languages while centering Christ. Let the island be a sending hub of spiritual vitality into the region, where missionary vision flows out from Palau and Agana to neighboring atolls. Strengthen small congregations with resources for discipleship so new converts are rooted and cultural practices that hinder faith are gently reformed.

Holy Spirit, fashion Guam into a model of unity in diversity: united in mission, peaceful in relationship, and powerful in outreach. I prophesy churches that sing together in many tongues, that serve together in mercy, and that disciple together in truth—bringing transformation to villages, towns, and the next generation. Let the bond of peace hold strong and the Kingdom advance across the Pacific.

In Jesus' name, Amen.

86

GUATEMALA

"And the things that you have heard from me among many witnesses, commit the same to faithful men, who shall be able to teach others also."
— 2 Timothy 2:2 WEB

Faithful Master and Builder of disciples, I stand before You for Guatemala and declare that the harvest already present will be firmly rooted by multiplication—leaders trained, disciples grounded, and churches maturing across Guatemala City, the highlands, and every indigenous community. I prophesy that the remarkable numerical growth among evangelicals will be accompanied by deep, reproducible discipleship so that converts become faithful teachers and leaders who in turn raise up others to teach and shepherd. Let the movement be one of quality as well as quantity.

Father, empower seminaries, Bible schools, and local training networks that contextualize doctrine for Spanish and Amerindian languages. Provide resources to translate and teach Scripture effectively in the many tongues across the nation. Equip pastors to resist prosperity distortions and syncretistic blends, teaching sound doctrine, biblical holiness, and robust pastoral care. Raise mentors who model Christlike humility and shepherding rather than self-promotion, ensuring leaders are multiplied with integrity.

Lord Jesus, bless the 25,000 congregations with structures for accountability and growth—small-group systems, discipleship curricula, and practical ministry projects that cultivate endurance. Multiply lay leaders, women leaders, and youth mentors who can operate in villages and cities alike, so that new converts never lack a local spiritual family. Encourage churches to invest in trauma care, economic development, and community reconciliation so the gospel heals both souls and societies.

Holy Spirit, release a wave of reproducible discipleship across Guatemala: faithful men and women trained to teach, multiplied churches maturing in doctrine and deed, and a nation where Christian growth results in transformed families and communities. I prophesy a Guatemala where revival is sustained through faithful transmission—where the gospel is passed hand to hand, heart to heart, into a future of deep and lasting fruit.

In Jesus' name, Amen.

87

GUINEA

"Train up a child in the way he should go; even when he is old he will not depart from it."
— Proverbs 22:6 WEB

Sovereign Lord, Teacher of the nations, I come as a guardian for Guinea and declare that the children and youth of Conakry and every village will be trained in the way of truth and life. I raise my voice for the millions under fifteen who need roots more than reform — and I call heaven's intensive discipleship to take hold. Where fear and uncertainty have chilled the land, let a fresh, patient investment in children and families by churches and Christian schools restore hope and resilience so that a whole generation grows into faithful, stable citizens.

Father, supply boldness and wisdom to the small but faithful Church in Guinea. Multiply the effectiveness of the three Bible schools and six leadership training centers so that they become factories of character: equipping pastors, teachers, and community workers who can disciple children and mentor young men and women into maturity. Protect young believers from spiritual erosion and the schemes of the enemy; grant perseverance, doctrinal truth, and wholesome community to those who are tempted to abandon faith in hard times. Let outreach flourish not as sporadic campaigns but as enduring relationships: children's ministries, after-school programs, literacy classes, and family discipleship that tangibly demonstrate the love of Christ.

Lord Jesus, move across the majority-Muslim regions with such incarnational love that barriers fall and hearts are opened. Use medical care, clean water projects, and vocational training to show the gospel in deed as well as word. Empower missionaries and local believers to work skillfully and culturally sensitively, loving neighbors in ways that gain trust and create openings for gospel proclamation. Raise indigenous leaders who can speak multiple languages — French, Fulbe, Malinke, Susu — and who will shepherd flocks across ethnic lines.

Holy Spirit, raise a movement of intercession and action in Guinea: prayer networks that support remote pastors, scholarship funds for faithful students, and restoration programs for families affected by instability. I prophesy that the seeds sown in the youth of Guinea will produce a harvest of godly leadership, stable families, and a church that endures. Let the training of children and the strengthening of leaders become the strategic turning point for this nation's future.

In Jesus' name, Amen.

88

Guinea-Bissau

"Pure and undefiled religion before God and the Father is this: to visit orphans and widows in their affliction, and to keep oneself unspotted from the world."
— James 1:27 WEB

Merciful Father and Defender of the helpless, I stand in the gap for Guinea-Bissau and call forth a wave of pure, active religion that tangibly blesses the poorest and most vulnerable. Where poverty, political unrest, and the corruption born of drug trafficking have bound the people in despair, I declare that the Church will act as Christ's hands and feet — visiting orphans, defending widows, supporting the displaced, and offering practical pathways out of dependency. Let the religion of words be replaced by the religion of rescuing the afflicted.

Father, raise righteous leaders who will break the cycle of instability and exploitation. Call out men and women of integrity into government, police, and civil institutions — leaders who will refuse bribes, prosecute traffickers, and build structures of fair justice. Empower reformers with courage and protection; dismantle corrupt networks that traffic drugs and recruit officials into compromises. Grant the judiciary and security forces godly convictions so they uphold the vulnerable rather than colluding with crime.

Lord Jesus, multiply compassionate ministries that provide education, literacy, and vocational training alongside gospel witness so the poor are not merely helped but transformed into contributors to society. Equip local churches to adopt orphan care, family restoration projects, and community savings schemes that create sustainable livelihood options. Enable international partners to support these efforts in ways that build local capacity rather than dependency.

Holy Spirit, sanctify the Church so believers keep themselves unspotted from worldliness even while serving in hard places. Release a holiness that resists compromise and a zeal that honours justice and mercy equally. I prophesy Guinea-Bissau arising from its burdens into a nation where the Church leads in both compassion and reform: children fed, widows protected, corrupt systems exposed, and a new generation trained for honest service. Let Your Kingdom come and righteous governance follow.

In Jesus' name, Amen.

89

Guyana

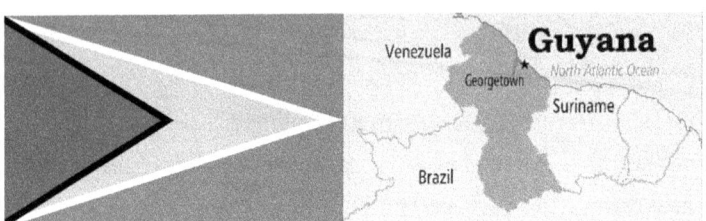

"Enlarge the place of your tent, and let them stretch forth the curtains of your habitations; spare not; lengthen your cords, and strengthen your stakes."
— Isaiah 54:2 WEB

Lord of territory and steward of every boundary, I bring Guyana before Your throne and prophesy an enlargement of the nation's stability, unity, and godly stewardship. Where land claims and political division threaten the body politic, I declare a widening of vision: economic protection for biodiversity, fair policies that prevent predatory exploitation, and political wisdom that binds racial divides with justice and reconciliation. Let Guyana's tents expand in security and dignity so that all people—Indo-Guyanese, Afro-Guyanese, Indigenous peoples—find room to prosper.

Father, grant wise statesmanship to those who steward the land and resources. Raise leaders who will negotiate borders with integrity, refuse unlawful encroachments, and contract with foreign companies in ways that prioritize local benefit and environmental care. Strengthen institutions that regulate exploitation and provide transparent revenue use so the nation avoids the curse of outside plunder. Provide incentives for talented nationals to remain or to return, creating opportunities at home for the gifted rather than forcing brain drain.

Lord Jesus, pour out a reconciling spirit between the major communities—healing historic wounds and promoting collaborative development projects that unite rather than divide. Empower churches and Christian leaders to model ethnic reconciliation with joint vocational programs, inter-ethnic schools, and community enterprises that employ across lines. Multiply gospel initiatives that reach the 18% unevangelized and the many unreached people groups with culturally sensitive witness and practical care.

Holy Spirit, strengthen the stakes of Guyana's civic fabric—justice, lawfulness, and environmental guardianship—so that the nation stands firm against exploitation and foreign encroachment. I prophesy a Guyana that stretches its cords wide in peace and purpose: a land where tents are enlarged for flourishing, where the gospel shapes public stewardship, and where the people together steward God's riches for the common good. Let Your Kingdom come across every river and forest.

In Jesus' name, Amen.

90

Haiti

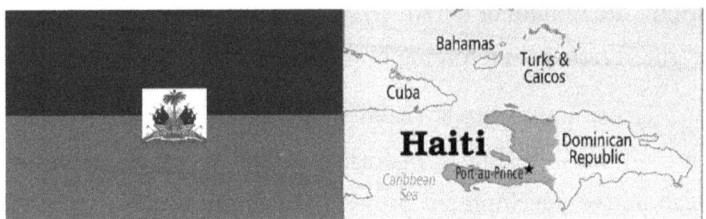

"For the weapons of our warfare are not carnal, but mighty through God to the pulling down of strongholds; bringing into captivity every thought to the obedience of Christ."
— 2 Corinthians 10:4–5 WEB

Mighty Conqueror and Deliverer, I come before You for Haiti and wield the spiritual weapons You have given us to tear down the webs of violence, voodoo strongholds, and generations of oppression. I prophesy the dismantling of demonic systems that undergird gang cruelty, sexual violence, and the cultural fear that has bound families for centuries. Let chains of spiritual bondage break now; may the minds and hearts of Haitians be brought captive to the truth of Christ so that fear gives way to faith, and tyranny yields to peace.

Father, release protection over towns and rural communities where armed gangs now rule. Empower local churches to be safe centers of refuge, providing food, trauma counseling, shelter, and hope. Raise and equip pastors and lay counselors with the skills to minister in crisis, and bless international partners who bring practical aid without exploiting vulnerability. Intervene to stop human trafficking and predatory exploitation tied to illegal mining and other dark trades; expose and dismantle networks that benefit from suffering.

Lord Jesus, pour out the Holy Spirit to cleanse the syncretistic mix of Christianity and voodoo by the power of life-changing testimony. Let the Church be purified: courageous, prophetic, and compassionate—leading the nation in repentance, mercy, and justice. Strengthen orphan care, vocational training, and agricultural initiatives that restore dignity and provide alternatives to gang enrollment. Empower churches to disciple in depth so that converts are not shallow but rooted in truth and virtue.

Holy Spirit, strengthen the people of Haiti with endurance and hope: heal the trauma of earthquakes, epidemics, political assassination, and economic collapse; restore families and rebuild communities. I prophesy a breaking of demonic strongholds, a spectacular movement of God's mercy, and the rise of a Haitian Church that shepherds a healed nation. Let the gospel be the power that transforms streets of fear into neighborhoods of worship and service.

In Jesus' name, Amen.

91

HOLY SEE (VATICAN CITY)

"A bishop then must be blameless, the husband of one wife, vigilant, sober-minded, of good behavior, given to hospitality, apt to teach."
— 1 Timothy 3:2 WEB

Heavenly Father, Shepherd of shepherds and Lord of the Church, I stand before You on behalf of the Holy See and prophesy that leaders will be raised who embody integrity, humility, and pastoral holiness. I ask that every shepherd in the Vatican and across the global Church be vigilant and sober-minded, given to hospitality, and seasoned in teaching truth with compassion. Let the papal office and the curia be led by men and women who pursue righteousness and who bear the weight of influence with servant-hearted devotion to the flock.

Father, grant the Pope and all Vatican leaders a spirit of discernment and pastoral courage as they navigate global upheaval, moral scandals, and the cries of the abused. Give them wisdom to institute reforms that protect children and vulnerable people, to bring transparent accountability, and to model restorative justice where harm has been done. Strengthen processes that uncover truth and bring healing, and bless the Church's global ministry with renewed credibility rooted in repentance and concrete protection for the wounded.

Lord Jesus, infuse the Holy See with the humility of Christ so that power is exercised as service. Let pastoral priorities lead administrative decisions; let missionary zeal shape diplomatic relations; let truth and charity guide theology and practice. Bless the Pope's voice with prophetic clarity and tender mercy that reaches rulers and refugees, clergy and laity alike. Guard him from exhaustion; surround him with faithful advisors who will counsel in truth and prayer.

Holy Spirit, renew the heart of the Roman See so that it stands as a source of healing and faithful witness to the world. I prophesy a Vatican where leaders are above reproach, policies protect the vulnerable, and the Church's lamp shines with both holiness and compassion. May the Holy See lead not by prestige alone but by sacrificial service, guiding the global body of Christ into greater faithfulness and mercy.

In Jesus' name, Amen.

92

Honduras

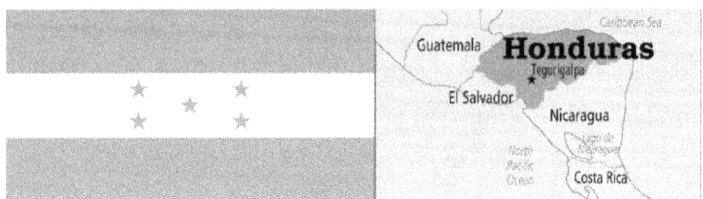

"He has told you, O man, what is good; and what does Yahweh require of you, but to do justice, and to love mercy, and to walk humbly with your God?"
— Micah 6:8 WEB

Sovereign Judge and Loving Father, I take my stand as a watchman over Honduras and prophetically declare that Your standards of justice, mercy, and humble dependence will shape the nation's next chapter. I lift Tegucigalpa and every barrio where children cry out in poverty and where gangs and cartels stalk the streets. I release the conviction of heaven that true national health is built on righteous systems, compassionate service, and a humble turning to You. Let the spirit of exploitation be exposed and replaced by a culture that prizes human dignity and seeks the flourishing of every child.

Father, move Your Church in Honduras to embody the threefold pathway of right living — to establish institutions and public practices that restore justice, to overflow with mercy for the most vulnerable, and to model dependence on Your wisdom rather than self-sufficient plans. Raise up leaders in government who will legislate fair wages, protect children from trafficking and exploitation, and prosecute those who use gangs to enslave youth. Let social policies center the welfare of families and children so that migration becomes a choice, not a desperate flight. Give planners creativity to provide alternative livelihoods and skills training that displace the economic incentives of criminal groups.

Lord Jesus, breathe spiritual courage into pastors, social workers, and community activists who risk everything to rescue children and to deliver youth from maras. Multiply counseling centers and AIDS-prevention ministries that are Christ-centered and evidence-based, and let them be present in schools, clinics, and neighborhoods. Equip the Church with medical outreach and public health initiatives that reduce HIV spread with dignity and care. Empower local congregations to be beacons of mercy: feeding programs, safe houses, mentoring, and pathways to honest employment that restore hope and break cycles of despair.

Holy Spirit, sweep across Honduras with revival that reshapes hearts and institutions alike. Let repentance, justice, and mercy converge so communities no longer tolerate corruption or violence. I prophesy schools filled with healthy children, neighborhoods where gang influence diminishes, and ministries that raise strong families — a Honduras where God's Kingdom comes in streets and policy, in homes and courts.

In Jesus' name, Amen.

93

HONG KONG

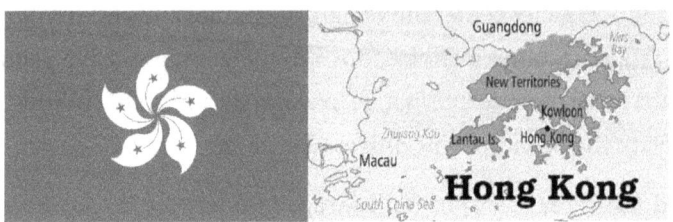

"Be strong and of good courage; do not be afraid, neither be dismayed: for Yahweh your God is with you wherever you go."
— Joshua 1:9 WEB

Mighty Lord and Ever-Present Helper, I stand as a bold intercessor over Hong Kong and declare that divine courage and God's abiding presence will anchor believers amid upheaval and migration. I prophetically release strength into the churches, into students, entrepreneurs, and families who face an uncertain future under shifting political realities. Where fear tempts flight and where the exodus of talent threatens the city's spiritual witness, I call heaven's steadiness so many will choose to stay and be salt and light, trusting that You walk with them in every public square, office, and home.

Father, empower remaining believers with resilient faith and creative Kingdom strategies. Grant pastors and lay leaders the wisdom to reconfigure ministry models—planting house fellowships, cultivating small group resilience, and training a wider base of disciples to shepherd one another. Let those who migrate carry mission vision rather than merely escape; may diaspora communities be strategic bridgeheads of prayer, advocacy, and resource flows back to Hong Kong. Provide governmental and societal openings where religious freedom can be exercised compassionately and with prudence.

Lord Jesus, fortify students and young professionals with conviction that honors peace while testifying to truth. Raise a generation that marries excellence in work with humble courage in witness—professionals who influence law, education, media, and arts without resorting to polarizing rhetoric. Bless ministries that serve the marginalized—migrants, domestic workers, the elderly—so the Church's compassion becomes a powerful apologetic. Protect those who must speak prophetically and give them words of wisdom grounded in love rather than merely ideology.

Holy Spirit, breathe supernatural boldness and calm into Hong Kong's body of believers. I prophesy pockets of faithful congregations remaining as bright beacons—creative, adaptive, and courageous—thus preserving a testimony that will draw many hearts. Let the city be known not for retreat but for a God-honoring perseverance that advances the Kingdom in small groups, workplaces, and public places.

In Jesus' name, Amen.

94

HUNGARY

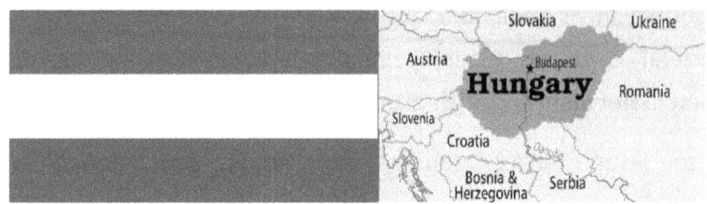

"And you will know the truth, and the truth will make you free."
— John 8:32 WEB

Lord Jesus, Lord of Truth and Light, I stand before You as an intercessor for Hungary and declare that Your liberating truth will displace deception, false mysticism, and every counterfeit that entices people into empty philosophies. I prophesy clarity to pierce the fog of occultism, Eastern mysticism, and syncretistic spiritualities that have drawn Hungarians away from gospel roots. Let the Word of God be taught with precision and applied with pastoral sensitivity so that Hungarians rediscover biblical reality as distinct from alluring but hollow alternatives.

Father, empower pastors and theological teachers to present sound doctrine with winsome cultural intelligence. Raise a cohort of well-trained leaders—scholars and street pastors alike—who can lovingly examine and expose false spiritualities, showing their poverty and leading people into the robust freedom of Christ. Support seminaries and training centers that marry deep biblical theology with practical pastoral care, equipping leaders to shepherd a people tempted by materialism and popularity of pagan practices.

Lord Jesus, stir a renewed hunger for authentic discipleship among families, students, and rural communities. Multiply small groups and mentorship programs that teach the Scriptures, model daily holiness, and demonstrate the fruit of a life submitted to Christ. Let Christian witness be credible through integrity in work, generosity in public life, and humility in leadership. Encourage believers to engage the arts, media, and education with truth, offering attractive alternatives to shallow spiritualities.

Holy Spirit, convict and convert where pride and curiosity have led astray. I prophesy Hungary reclaiming its Christian heritage with renewed authenticity—a nation where truth brings freedom, communities reject deceptive rituals, and the Church stands courageous and winsome. Let the light of Christ dismantle darkness and bring a people into lasting liberty.

In Jesus' name, Amen.

95

ICELAND

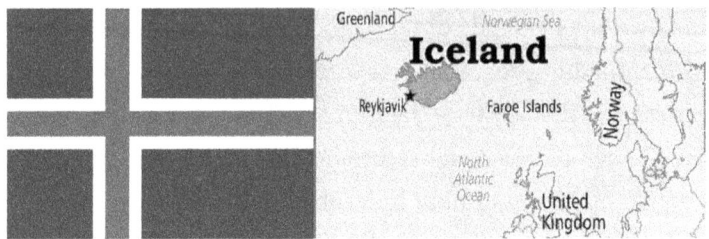

"O Yahweh, how manifold are your works! In wisdom you have made them all; the earth is full of your riches."
— Psalm 104:24 WEB

Creator God, Sovereign Artist of mountain and sea, I lift Iceland before Your throne and declare that this nation—rich in natural beauty and fraught with new material temptations—will steward its gifts with wisdom that honors You. I prophesy that leaders and citizens will be guided by a reverence for Your creative handiwork and by practical prudence in decisions over land use, resource development, and immigration. Let economic gain never eclipse the responsibility to preserve the environment and to protect the vulnerable who live within these places of breathtaking beauty.

Father, grant political leaders and planners godly wisdom to balance conservation with development. Provide wise policies that protect fisheries, glacial lands, and unique ecosystems while creating sustainable livelihoods for communities. Help legislators to listen to indigenous and local voices, to anticipate long-term ecological consequences, and to design frameworks that prevent short-term profit from undermining generational flourishing. Bless research and innovation that return value to local families and prevent exploitative foreign ventures.

Lord Jesus, stir the Church into creative expressions that address both spiritual thirst and civic responsibility. Empower congregations to lead in environmental stewardship, community integration for immigrants, and compassionate care for those suffering social dislocation. Encourage theological reflection that lovingly engages modernity—teaching that faith does not fear science but is enriched by awe for creation, and that stewardship is integral to discipleship.

Holy Spirit, renew wonder in the Icelandic heart so that gratitude for God's manifold works fuels both protection and welcome. I prophesy a nation where leaders govern with godly foresight, where communities unite around beauty and justice, and where the gospel informs both conservation and hospitality. Let Iceland be an example of careful stewardship, cultural wisdom, and spiritual curiosity rooted in the Creator.

In Jesus' name, Amen.

96

INDIA

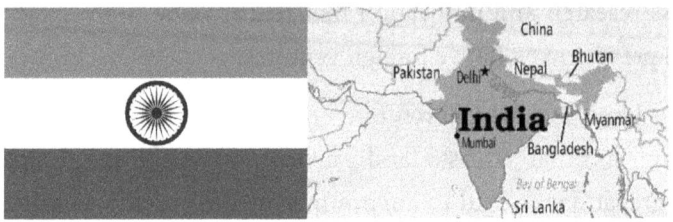

"The harvest truly is plenteous, but the laborers are few."
— Matthew 9:37 WEB

Lord of the nations and Master of the harvest, I come before You on behalf of India and declare that the vast fields of souls will be met with multiplied laborers, deep discipleship, and courageous compassion. I lift New Delhi and the teeming cities, remote villages, tribal homelands, and every unreached town; I prophesy an unprecedented mobilization of workers—indigenous, sent, and trained—who will humbly enter these fields with cultural sensitivity, bold love, and theological depth. Let Your mercy move across caste, creed, and region to bring healing and the clear proclamation of Christ.

Father, provide abundant resources for training indigenous leaders so that seminaries and Bible schools multiply contextualized models for ministry. Raise teachers competent in local languages, effective in pastoral care, and rooted in Scripture; equip them to work among Dalits, tribal peoples, urban middle classes, and higher castes alike. Break down caste prejudice within the Church; let Christians model radical equality and bring the love of Christ to those historically oppressed. Strengthen networks that send and sustain missionaries into the vast unreached communities, especially in Uttar Pradesh, Odisha, and the tribal heartlands.

Lord Jesus, protect Your people from rising persecution and grant wisdom to navigate hostile contexts without compromise. Empower house-church movements and discipling rhythms that make believers mature and resilient. Multiply mercy ministries that target the most vulnerable—women and children trapped in abuse, exploited minors, orphans, and those consigned to trafficking—so the Church becomes a shelter and a force for systemic change: education, vocational training, rescue, and legal advocacy.

Holy Spirit, breathe revival over India that brings both numbers and depth: mass movements rooted in repentance, sound doctrine, and social transformation. I prophesy that the harvest will be reaped through cooperative global and local efforts—media, audio Scripture, radio, contextual literature, and trained laborers—so that the light of Christ pierces regions long darkened. Raise laborers, sustain them, protect them, and let the gospel make India a place where dignity, freedom, and faith flourish together.

In Jesus' name, Amen.

97

INDONESIA

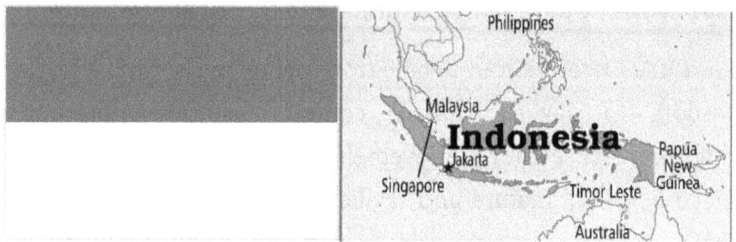

"You are the light of the world. A city set on a hill cannot be hidden."
— Matthew 5:14 WEB

Sovereign Light of the Nations, I stand before You as an intercessor for Indonesia and I declare in faith that Your Church in Jakarta, Java, Sumatra, Kalimantan, Sulawesi, Bali, Maluku and Papua will shine forth as a city on a hill. I prophesy that where darkness of occult practices, persecution, cultural displacement, and spiritual strongholds have threatened to overwhelm entire people groups, the radiance of Christ will break through. I ask that believers who are small in number but mighty in spirit will be raised up as visible lights — communities of love, courage, and glad witness that cannot be hidden.

I pray for governmental wisdom and mercy where relocation and resettlement policies have sown deep wounds among indigenous peoples. I plead that ministries of compassion will be empowered to accompany displaced families — housing, culturally sensitive counseling, legal advocacy and fair land agreements — so the pain of marginalization is met with justice. I declare that laws which restrict church building and persecute sincere believers will be restrained, and that the Spirit will give church leaders prophetic strategy to navigate restrictions while planting reproducible fellowships. Let the harvest in Java and the openness in pockets of Sulawesi and Sumatra be mobilized into intentional outreach to the 233 least-reached peoples.

I ask Father to deepen discipleship so that growth becomes maturity. I call training for pastors, Bible translators and lay-workers to be multiplied — teams fluent in local tongues who can translate Scripture, lead house churches, and confront syncretism with love and truth. Raise indigenous aviation, medical and logistical ministries that reach remote Kalimantan and Papua; multiply Scripture storying and audio Bible efforts where literacy and language are barriers. Strengthen new believers from Muslim backgrounds with strong mentoring and safe fellowship so whole households turn to Christ with endurance.

Holy Spirit, release a revival that combines compassion with courage: churches that feed, teach, heal, translate and proclaim. I prophesy that Indonesian believers — diverse in ethnicity and language — will exhibit Christlike love so attractively that whole villages, even islands, come to know Jesus. Let the light of Christ make all darkness flee and let the Kingdom come across every island and tribe. In Jesus' name, Amen.

98

IRAN

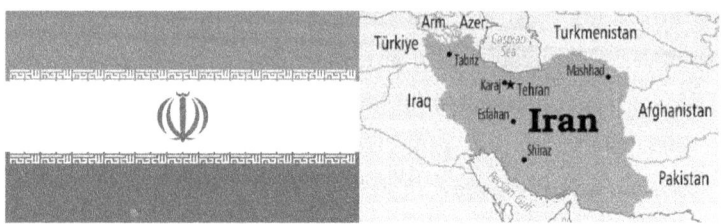

"I will give you a new heart, and a new spirit I will put within you; and I will take away the stony heart out of your flesh, and I will give you a heart of flesh."
— Ezekiel 36:26 WEB

Sovereign Redeemer and Giver of New Life, I lift Iran before Your throne and I declare that You are at work in Persian hearts. I pray in the authority of heaven for a profound renewal—an inward transformation that removes hardness and replaces it with tender devotion to Jesus. I prophesy that the millions who have privately turned to Christ will be sustained with supernatural courage, that hidden communities will be knit by love, and that hearts once cold will be warmed by encounters with Your living presence.

I ask for protection and wisdom for believers in Tehran, Isfahan, Mashhad, and across the mountains and plains. Where apostasy laws and persecution threaten, clothe Your people in discernment and grant them strategic, safe ways to worship, disciple and serve. Strengthen underground networks of house churches and training hubs; enable the distribution of Scripture in Persian and provide creative means of theological education that cannot be easily suppressed. Let dreams, visions, and signs continue to draw many, accompanied by solid teaching so converts are grounded and mature.

Father, bring ministry resources that heal trauma and restore dignity — pastoral counseling, literacy and vocational training that enable families to flourish. Raise international and regional partners who will stand with Iranian believers in prayer, advocacy, and practical support without compromising safety. Empower the Church to be a quiet agent of mercy among neighbors — providing medical care, relief and hospitality — so that Christ's love opens doors across social and ethnic lines.

Holy Spirit, accomplish in Iran what only You can: convicting power, secrecy for protection, boldness for witness, and long-term stability for the Church. I prophesy an ongoing movement where many from Muslim, Zoroastrian and other backgrounds find a transformed heart and steadfast faith — a Persia renewed by the Spirit, walking in humility and truth.

In Jesus' name, Amen.

99

IRAQ

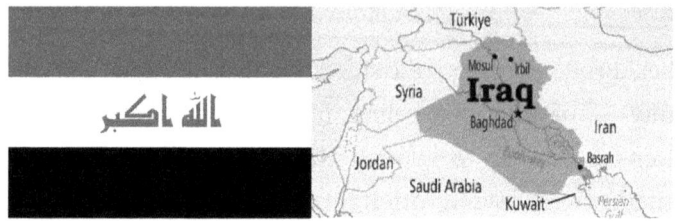

"The Spirit of the Lord Yahweh is on me; because Yahweh has anointed me to preach good news to the humble; he has sent me to bind up the brokenhearted..."
— Isaiah 61:1 WEB

Lord Messiah, Healer of broken places, I stand as an intercessor over Iraq and I declare that Your anointing rests on the emerging Iraqi Church. I lift Baghdad, Mosul, Kurdistan, and every devastated region and prophesy that the Lord's appointed work of preaching good news, binding wounds, and proclaiming liberty will be fulfilled. May the young evangelicals and those who have found Christ in dreams be equipped not only to survive but to lead healing movements across their towns, bringing restoration to families ravaged by war and fear.

I plead for God's justice to dismantle the violent networks that have ruled by terror. Where militias and extremist groups have profited from chaos, I ask for governmental reform, fair rule of law, and protective measures that return civil life to neighborhoods. Raise trustworthy leaders who will champion reconciliation and rebuild infrastructure, hospitals, and schools. Grant security forces wisdom that distinguishes genuine protection from abuse, and provide resettlement and trauma care so displaced communities can return to a dignified life.

Lord Jesus, empower pastors, elders and widows who carry on the work of discipling and feeding the hungry. Multiply Bible teaching, contextual discipleship, and theological training so new believers are grounded and can lead with courage. Strengthen networks of women ministers and those who care for children orphaned by conflict so the next generation grows up with love rather than hatred. Let churches be sanctuaries of peace where ethnically mixed congregations practice forgiveness and mutual support.

Holy Spirit, breathe patience and prophetic endurance across Iraq. I prophesy a people who rise from rubble to plant churches, rebuild schools, and proclaim good news; I see communities restored, testimonies multiplying, and a generation living in liberty under Christ's lordship. May the anointing for healing and freedom sweep over this land.

In Jesus' name, Amen.

100

IRELAND

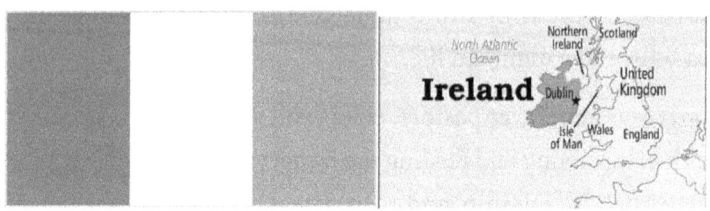

"If my people, who are called by my name, shall humble themselves, and pray, and seek my face, and turn from their wicked ways; then will I hear from heaven, and will forgive their sin, and will heal their land."
— 2 Chronicles 7:14 WEB

Holy and Compassionate God, I stand before You on behalf of Ireland and declare that genuine repentance and restorative healing will come to the Church and the nation. I prophesy that the wounds opened by abuse and cover-up will be met with sincere contrition, transparent justice and pastoral reformation. Let the cleansing work begin at the highest levels of church leadership and cascade into parishes and families so that trust can be rebuilt and the Gospel again be offered with integrity.

I ask for deep humility among ecclesial leaders: confessing sin, making restitution, and cooperating fully with civil authorities to bring perpetrators to justice. Pour courage into clerical and lay reformers to implement safeguarding reforms, to prioritize victims, and to transform institutions into places of safety. Give government and church collaborative structures that ensure accountability and support for survivors — counseling, legal aid, and restorative processes that are both just and merciful.

Lord Jesus, renew the Irish laity with thoughtful faith and spiritual hunger; raise small communities of discipleship that practice transparency, prayer, and mutual care. Multiply ministries that equip families, teach children emotional and spiritual resilience, and prepare pastors to lead with pastoral competence rather than mere administrative authority. Let a wave of theological renewal combine humility with robust teaching so the faithful can again find a living Christ in place of empty ritual.

Holy Spirit, bring a national healing that honors victims and transforms institutions. I prophesy an Ireland where repentance births renewed trust, where the Church is purified and becomes a credible witness of grace, and where communities flourish in holiness and compassion. May the land be healed by truth and the Gospel's renewing power.

In Jesus' name, Amen.

101

ISRAEL

"Pray for the peace of Jerusalem: May those who love you prosper. May there be peace within your ramparts."
— Psalm 122:6 WEB

God of Abraham, Isaac and Jacob, Keeper of covenant promises, I lift Israel — Jerusalem, Tel Aviv, the Galilee, and the communities across the land — before Your throne and I call for Your mercy. I stand as a believer pleading for peace and I declare that Your compassion must overshadow bitterness and vengeance. In the midst of war, grief and deep political division I release an urgent cry that both hearts and leaders will seek the God of justice who alone can bind wounds and supernaturally incline leaders toward ceasefire, restitution and reconciliation.

I pray for protection and provision for ordinary citizens — Jews, Arabs, Druze, Bedouins, and Christians — who suffer under violence and fear. Soften the hearts of political and military leaders toward humane and just solutions that protect civilians and dismantle networks of terror. Where hatred and cycles of retaliation have hardened communities, disarm the spirit of vengeance and replace it with a hunger for lasting peace and restorative justice. Let humanitarian corridors open and aid reach the most desperate.

Lord Jesus, strengthen the small but faithful Arab Christian witness and the minority of believers among Jews; equip them as salt and light who mediate mercy and reconciliation. Raise prophetic voices within both communities that call for repentance, practical reconciliation projects, and cross-cultural partnerships — rebuilding homes, schools, and interfaith initiatives that model mutual flourishing. Bless ministries that care for victims of trauma, the displaced, widows and orphans with professional counseling and gospel hope.

Holy Spirit, pour out a divine restraint on violent hearts and a supernatural inclination toward peace. I prophesy openings for dialogue, extraordinary displays of compassion that surprise enemies, and grassroots movements that bind the city's wounds. Let prayer for Jerusalem bring peace to the ramparts and let Your Kingdom purpose move powerfully among nations involved.

In Jesus' name, Amen.

102

ITALY

"Is not this the fast that I have chosen: to loosen the bands of wickedness, to undo the heavy burdens, and to let the oppressed go free, and that you break every yoke?"
— Isaiah 58:6–7 WEB

Righteous Judge and Liberator, I stand before You for Italy and declare that the powers of organized crime, corruption, and spiritual bondage will be exposed and broken. I prophesy that the "heavy burdens" carried by families and communities under the sway of mafias and exploitative systems will be loosened. Let courageous men and women arise in law enforcement, judiciary, civil society, and the Church who will not flinch in the face of intimidation but who pursue justice, protect the vulnerable, and restore what was stolen.

I pray for bold, godly leadership to confront entrenched criminal networks — the Mafia, Camorra, 'Ndrangheta — and for the legal system to function with integrity and protection for whistleblowers. Empower prosecutors, judges, and honest public servants with divine wisdom and safety so they can enact reforms that cut off the economic arteries of organized crime. Bless anti-corruption movements and support them with public awareness campaigns, economic alternatives for exploited communities, and vigorous enforcement.

Lord Jesus, renew the Church in Italy with prophetic courage and pastoral authenticity so believers resist the temptations of compromise and syncretism. Raise pastors who preach repentance and social righteousness, and churches that model transparency and sacrificial service. Equip Christian NGOs to reach those drawn to occult and New Age practices with relational witness, mercy ministries and clear teaching about the true gospel, inviting people from Turin to Sicily into restored faith.

Holy Spirit, bring deliverance and a national reformation of heart: break yokes of fear and poverty, free victims from cycles of abuse, and cause communities to rebuild with dignity and justice. I prophesy Italy emerging from the shadow of criminal influence into a season where the oppressed are freed, stolen goods are restored in spirit, and the light of Christ shines upon public life. Let Your kingdom rule over the boot of Italy.

In Jesus' name, Amen.

103

Jamaica

"Enlarge the place of your tent, and let them stretch out the curtains of your habitations: spare not, lengthen your cords, and strengthen your stakes; For you will spread abroad to the right and to the left; and your seed will inherit the nations, and will people the desolate cities."
— Isaiah 54:2–3 WEB

O Sovereign God, King over heaven and earth, I lift up Jamaica as a fragrant offering before Your throne. O Lord of the harvest, move like a mighty wind over Kingston, Montego Bay, and every ridge and parish — extend the tent of Your presence across every shore. I declare that the heritage of missionary sending, the zeal of revival, and the Bible-rich legacy of this island will not be wasted but will be enlarged and strengthened. I call forth the strengthening of leaders in Bible societies, seminaries, and Keswick assemblies — let cords be lengthened, stakes driven deep, and foundations secured in gospel truth.

Father, I intercede for every Bible school, seminary, and Keswick conference — the 15 centers of training and the ministries that steward Scripture — that they become impregnable citadels of sound doctrine and godly living. Raise professors and pastors who embody holiness and humility; send students hungry for Scripture and courageous in mission. Let every classroom and chapel be a birthplace of missionaries, evangelists, and compassionate servants who will carry Jamaica's flame to the Caribbean, to cities and to peoples who hunger for truth. Turn resources, finances, and influence toward training the next generation; let stewardship be marked by integrity and joyful giving.

Lord Jesus, for the young people — the special vision of the Bible Society — I cry out for innovative gospel engagement. Rescue children and teenagers from the snares of poverty, addiction, and cultural confusion. Baptize youth movements with courage to worship, to serve, and to lead. Where there has been complacency, send fresh conviction; where churches are well-resourced, send humility and a missionary heart to bless neighboring islands and nations. Let Jamaican evangelicals and historic churches move as one, not for prestige, but to fulfill the Great Commission with creativity and compassion.

Almighty God, break any spirit of territorialism or ungodly influence that keeps people from hearing the gospel. Prosper godly leaders who govern churches and parachurch ministries with wisdom. Release a season of multiplication — of churches, Bible distribution, and missions — so that desolate places within the region are repopulated with gospel light. By Your Spirit, cause

Jamaica to be recognized not only for culture and song but as a strategic sending center saturated with prayer, Scripture, and holiness. I claim the inheritance You promised: the spreading of gospel seed to the right and to the left, until the nations see Your glory. In Jesus' name, Amen.

104

Japan

"If my people, who are called by my name, will humble themselves, and pray and seek my face, and turn from their wicked ways; then will I hear from heaven, and will forgive their sin, and will heal their land."
— 2 Chronicles 7:14 WEB

Majestic Lord, Author of life and Sustainer of nations, I stand in the gap for Japan and cry out for a national turning. I declare that the God who made the islands and set the sun will not be silent while hearts wander in ritual and emptiness. I call for humility to arise among those who bear Your name in Japan — for churches, seminaries, and scattered believers to entwine their knees in fasting and fervent intercession. Raise up a new generation of humble, praying disciples who seek Your face and catalyze a movement of genuine repentance and hope across this nation.

Compassionate Redeemer, shine Your light into the places of greatest need: the lonely, depressed, isolated elderly, and struggling youth. Where suicide, loneliness, and social despair have become normalized, send rescue in the form of Christian community, hospices, and care ministries. Let Christian nursing homes, counseling centers, and faith-based social services multiply, offering dignity and gospel care to an aging society. Equip missionaries and Japanese believers to enter schools, workplaces, and neighborhoods with practical compassion and faithful witness, opening doors where social systems cannot reach.

Lord of wisdom, dethrone the spiritual powers that veil hearts: the ancestral rituals, the spirits of delusion, and the false attractions of new religions. Break the grip of idolatries entrenched in temple and home, and loosen chains of superstition that keep people from the knowledge of the Creator. I ask for revelation to spring up among the unreached — that those who think the idea of a Creator is foreign may meet Jesus in dreams, conversations, and acts of sacrificial love. Empower the small but faithful churches to be beacons of truth and places of refuge for seekers and the marginalized.

Almighty God, grant strategic favor to the Church's engagement with culture: give believers creativity to speak hope into education, mental health, arts, and public life. Stir hearts among Japanese youth (ages 18–23) to become active disciples, not merely curious observers. Send revival to campuses, workplaces, and families so that what began as small and hidden will expand and bear fruit for generations. We declare healing for the land — healed relationships, healed communities, healed souls — that Japan might be a people renewed under Your rule. In Jesus' name, Amen.

105

Jordan

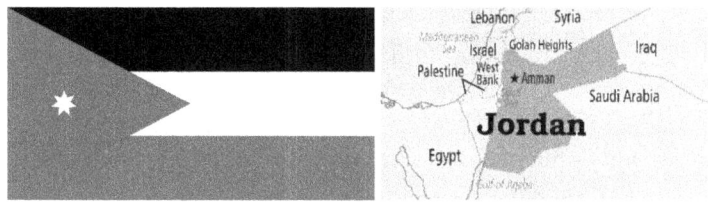

> "Thus says the LORD of hosts, 'Seek the welfare of the city where I have caused you to be carried away captives, and pray to the LORD for it; for in its welfare you will have welfare.'"
> — Jeremiah 29:7 WEB

Sovereign Lord of mercy and defender of the weak, I come before You on behalf of Jordan — a nation bearing heavy burdens yet set as a watchman in a volatile region. I lift King Abdullah, the government, and every leader into Your hands; grant them wisdom like that of Solomon and hearts that pursue justice and compassion. I pray for political steadiness and for policies that protect both Jordanian citizens and the many refugees who find shelter within its borders. Let the government act with integrity, fairness, and a servant spirit that honors the image of Christ.

Compassionate Father, bless the Christian minority in Jordan — the faithful women and men who serve quietly in hospitals, schools, and public life. Strengthen their witness, enlarge their influence, and protect them from persecution and marginalization. Let evangelical communities, traditional churches, and believers from Muslim backgrounds cooperate in humility and courage to plant churches, run relief efforts, and stand as salt and light in neighborhoods. Multiply avenues for training and discipleship so new believers can mature and serve their nation with excellence.

Lord of peace, pour supernatural protection over the cities and borderlands. Silence the schemes of violent extremists and dismantle trafficking networks and the forces that bring murder and fear. Bind the spirits of violence and vengeance; release the spirit of reconciliation and public order. Pour out Your compassion on the displaced — provide housing, work, education, and dignity — and open the hearts of Jordanian society to receive both refugees and gospel ministry as a blessing, not a burden.

Heavenly King, let Jordan become a regional hub of Christian activity that cannot be shaken. Empower seminaries, aid organizations, and intercessory networks to flourish. Convert adversity into mission opportunity: let the suffering and displacement awaken seekers and cause the gospel to proliferate through acts of mercy and the faithful witness of Christ's followers. May the welfare of Jordan be established so that its people — refugees and citizens alike — share in peace, prosperity, and the knowledge of God's reign. In Jesus' name, Amen.

106

KAZAKHSTAN

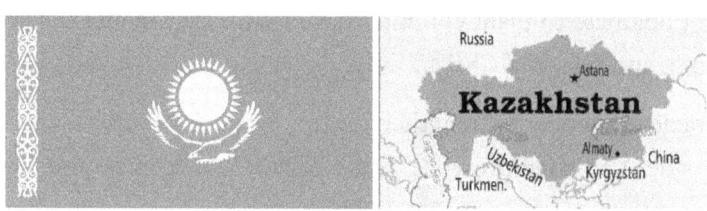

"First of all, then, I exhort that supplications, prayers, intercessions, and giving of thanks be made for all men; For kings, and for all who are in authority; that we may lead a quiet and peaceable life in all godliness and gravity."
— 1 Timothy 2:1–2 WEB

Lord God, Ruler of nations, I bow before You for Kazakhstan, a land of abundant resources and strategic significance. I cry aloud for servant leadership to arise — presidents, governors, parliamentarians and local officials who will govern with justice, resist corruption, and steward natural wealth for the common good. Break the spirit of greed that hoards resources for the few; bring transparency to institutions and systems so that pipelines of wealth become channels of blessing for health, education, and the vulnerable.

Mighty Deliverer, touch the religious and spiritual identity of this nation. Where cultural identity has fused national belonging with a version of Islam mixed with shamanic practice, speak a new narrative of spiritual freedom. Remove the chains of historic bondages, ancestral spirits, and false religious investment that prevent many from hearing the gospel clearly. Open hearts among ethnic Kazakhs and Russians alike, and grant the Church creativity and boldness to plant communities of faith that model the love, truth, and power of Christ.

Gracious Shepherd, strengthen the tiny evangelical witness and the broader Christian presence; equip pastors, evangelists, and small house churches to persevere under pressure and to be witnesses of righteousness. Send missionaries and church planters with cultural wisdom to serve in hospitals, schools, and rural communities where the gospel can be enacted through service. Raise up Christian leaders who can offer alternatives to corruption—models of business integrity, accountable leadership, and sacrificial generosity.

Holy Spirit, pour out renewal over families and youth, reversing spiritual drift and indifference. Empower discipleship movements that cultivate mature believers who influence media, education, and public life. I pray for policies that respect freedom of conscience and religious expression, and for a cultural shift that values truth and mercy. Let Kazakhstan's lands and people be restored to flourishing under Your just and loving rule, so that the nation becomes a place where peace, prosperity, and the fear of the Lord multiply. In Jesus' name, Amen.

107

KENYA

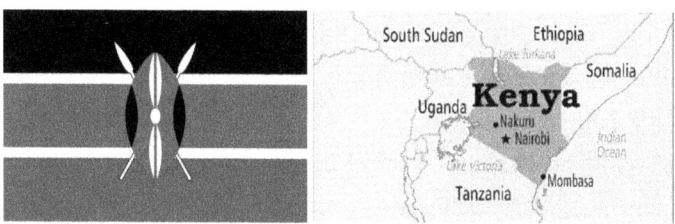

"But let justice run down as waters, and righteousness as a mighty stream."
— Amos 5:24 WEB

Lord of justice and mercy, I stand in the breach for Kenya — for Nairobi and every county, for slum and field, for the children in shanties and the elders in remote villages. I call upon You to dethrone corruption and to let justice pour forth like life-giving water into parched places. Raise judges, leaders, and public servants who love righteousness, who protect the poor, and who punish the wicked. Stir the conscience of those in power to enact land reform, fight graft, and defend the vulnerable with courage that honors Your name.

Heavenly Father, bind the spirits that foment ethnic hatred and violence over land and resources. Where tribalism has become a tool of division, pour out Your reconciling Spirit to unite communities around the common good. Equip the Church — the massive evangelical presence across denominations — to be an agent of societal transformation: to provide honest leadership, to expose corruption, and to offer practical solutions for poverty, sanitation, and sustainable agriculture. Let Pentecostal zeal be tempered with wisdom and justice, producing tangible change in people's daily lives.

Compassionate Savior, bless initiatives that bring schooling, healthcare, and clean water to slums and rural villages. Multiply faithful NGOs, churches, and Christian entrepreneurs who create jobs, build homes, and restore dignity. Protect Kenya from the influence of terrorists and traffickers by strengthening law enforcement guided by integrity and by communities united in vigilance. Raise prophetic voices in the pulpit and the marketplace that call the nation to repentance, charity, and wise stewardship.

Lord Jesus, kindle unity among Christians so they move beyond denominational rivalry into collaborative action for policy reform and public accountability. Let faith shape legislation that honors human dignity and punishes exploitation. Release a season where gospel truth transforms institutions, where righteousness flows through courts and councils like a mighty stream. I declare that Kenya's abundant spiritual resources and fervent people will not be wasted but will rise as instruments of national healing and godly prosperity. In Jesus' name, Amen.

108

KIRIBATI

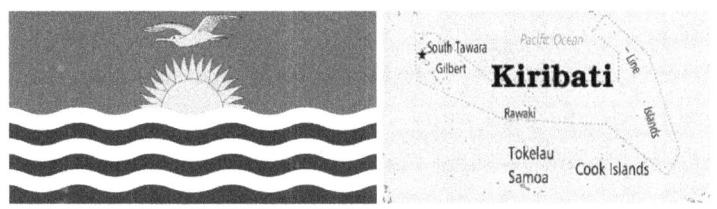

"Your word is a lamp to my feet, and a light to my path."
— Psalm 119:105 WEB

Sovereign Lord, Word made flesh and Light of the islands, I come before Your throne as a watchman for Kiribati and declare that Your Word will again be the lamp that guides Tarawa and every atoll. I prophesy a return from nominalism and syncretism into a vibrant, Bible-centered faith: congregations that sing with conviction, families reoriented around Scripture, and pastors trained to preach and disciple with clarity. Let the theological college on Tarawa be renewed by Your Spirit so it becomes a fountain of Scripture-saturated leaders who will not merely manage churches but form disciples for life.

Father, displace the mixture of spiritist practices that has compromised devotion with the pure gospel. Replace superstition with sound doctrine and pastoral care that addresses the real spiritual and social needs of the people. Provide resources for contextual Bible teaching in the local tongue, and bless adult classes, children's ministries, and youth outreaches that restore theological literacy across island life. Raise a generation of teachers and evangelists who will traverse atolls and villages carrying both Word and compassion so that small congregations are revived into soul-nurturing communities.

Lord Jesus, grant humility to existing church leadership so they will embrace godly reform rather than defensive preservation. Anoint pastors with pastoral fruit—patience, courage, doctrinal fidelity and compassion—so that the Church's witness becomes credible to a culture caught between tradition and modernity. Let the 7.2% evangelical minority be a catalytic presence, not sectarian but open-handed, partnering with the historic Protestant bodies to renew worship, restore discipleship, and strengthen families against immorality and cultural drift.

Holy Spirit, breathe revival across the coral atolls: bring conversions, sanctifying power, and sustained renewal that outlives a moment. I prophesy Kiribati rising as a light among the Pacific islands—clear in doctrine, tender in witness, and enduring in faith—so that the Word truly becomes lamp and path for every believer.

In Jesus' name, Amen.

109

Kosovo

"They devoted themselves to the apostles' teaching and the fellowship, to the breaking of bread and the prayers."
— Acts 2:42 WEB

Mighty Lord and Gatherer of the scattered, I lift Kosovo before Your throne and declare that the young, evangelistic churches across Pristina and smaller towns will deepen into lasting, reproducing communities. I prophesy that the fervor that has birthed growth will be matched by devotion to sound teaching, committed fellowship, sacramental life and fervent prayer. Let these components become the DNA of the Evangelical Movement of Kosovo so that numbers increase with spiritual maturity, not merely with nominal counts.

Father, strengthen unity among believers who worship in different languages and come from varied backgrounds. Where persecution and cultural pressure make discipleship costly—especially for girls and women—grant courage, wise protection, and creative pathways for secret and public discipleship. Raise seasoned teachers and mentors from the current youthful body—men and women who can guide younger believers into theological depth, pastoral skill, and missional imagination.

Lord Jesus, multiply networks of care that sustain pastors who are often young and under-resourced. Provide seminaries and short-term training programs that fit the local context, equipping leaders in evangelism, counseling, and church planting. Let the 35 evangelical churches not be isolated islands but linked through mutual accountability, joint outreach campaigns, and shared resources so that a national movement matures into a robust, responsible church family that can face societal pressures together.

Holy Spirit, release perseverance and holiness over Kosovo's churches so that this fragile, emerging body will be established and multiplied into generations. I prophesy a Church that stands firm amid ethnic tensions, that welcomes the persecuted, and that becomes a stabilizing moral influence—bringing hope, reconciliation and spiritual depth to a young nation.

In Jesus' name, Amen.

110

KUWAIT

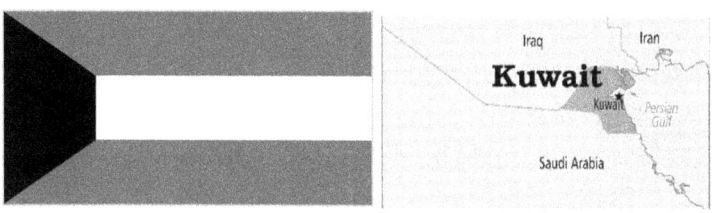

"You shall love the stranger, for you were strangers in the land of Egypt."
— Leviticus 19:34 WEB

Compassionate Father and Refuge of the weary, I stand in prayer for Kuwait and declare that Your heart for the foreign workers and the lonely will be made manifest in homes and churches across the emirate. I prophesy a rising compassion among believers—expatriate congregations and local families alike—that will reach into the lives of houseworkers, migrants, and men separated from families by necessity. Let ministries of hospitality, legal support, and dignified care flourish so that many who are lonely find family, fairness, and the living Christ.

Father, open the eyes of employers, community leaders, and church networks to the plight and potential of these workers. Move civic and religious leaders to defend human dignity, to remove unjust treatment, and to sponsor programs that teach language, rights, and vocational empowerment. Strengthen the Christian minority with wise cultural engagement so the witness of compassion becomes a credible light to Kuwaiti neighbors.

Lord Jesus, bless those Christians laboring under foreign stress with resilience and faithful witness. Multiply gospel opportunities within homes and workplaces—small Bible studies, English classes with hospitality, medical care and trauma counseling—that invite hearts to Christ without coercion. Provide protective legal avenues and safe outlets for reporting injustice so that exploitation is reduced and restoration increases.

Holy Spirit, bind isolation with community; turn loneliness into fellowship and injustice into advocacy. I prophesy that Kuwait's expatriate believers will be a powerful, prayerful presence—bringing mercy into homes, justice into workplaces, and the gospel into hearts across languages and cultures. Let the love of Christ transform labor camps, mansions, and marketplaces into arenas of compassionate testimony.

In Jesus' name, Amen.

111

Kyrgyzstan

"Defend the poor and fatherless; do justice to the afflicted and needy."
— Psalm 82:3 WEB

Sovereign Judge and Protector of the vulnerable, I take Kyrgyzstan before Your throne and declare that the poor, the aged, and the marginalized of Bishkek and mountain villages will find defenders in the Church and justice in the land. I prophesy that Christians who are dispersed among slums and migrating communities will be raised up as agents of social renewal—establishing legal help, job-training, addiction recovery, and community care that tangibly resist corruption and crime. Let righteousness shape public life so that those exploited by trafficking, gambling and vice find mercy and a pathway out.

Father, empower believers to model integrity in workplaces and to found institutions that offer legal, medical and vocational support.

Raise entrepreneurs who will create fair employment and apprenticeships for those fleeing rural poverty, ensuring migrants can find lawful, dignified work. Strengthen anti-corruption reforms and the courage of public servants who will stand against graft in police and government. Provide resources and international partnerships to fund recovery centers for alcoholism, drug rehabilitation, and shelters for exploited women and children.

Lord Jesus, equip the Church with pastoral resources to address spiritual and social brokenness: trained counselors, trauma-informed ministries, and discipleship pathways for the many youth and displaced families. Multiply small groups that disciple while equipping practical life skills—financial literacy, parenting classes, and vocational mentorship—so believers become citizens who bless their towns and influence public morality.

Holy Spirit, bring a movement of justice and compassion across Kyrgyzstan that heals slums, creates dignified jobs, and reforms corrupted systems. I prophesy communities where the poor are defended, the addicted are restored, and the Church stands as a beacon of integrity and mercy—so the nation's streets and institutions reflect the justice of heaven.

In Jesus' name, Amen.

112

LAOS

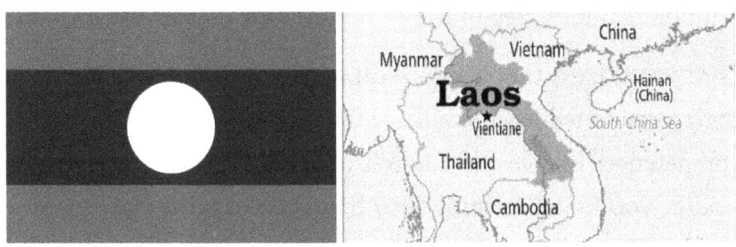

"He who began a good work in you will complete it until the day of Jesus Christ."
— Philippians 1:6 WEB

Faithful Sustainer and Finisher of every work, I present Laos before Your throne and declare that the rapid growth of the Church, though pressured, is a work You will complete. I prophesy stability for house churches and recognized denominations across Vientiane, the highlands, and remote villages: new believers rooted in sound teaching, trained leaders returning or emerging locally, and a mature Church that perseveres under pressure. Let the small, faithful congregations become multiplying centers of discipleship that withstand persecution and produce enduring fruit.

Father, provide practical training and resources for the many congregations that lack trained pastors. Multiply indigenous leaders through short-term intensives, contextual Bible schools, and mentoring that is safe and sustainable under current restrictions. Protect emerging leaders from burnout and persecution; give them wisdom in ministry, skills in discipleship, and networks of encouragement so they can shepherd without crumbling under pressure.

Lord Jesus, bless the recognized Lao Evangelical Church and the underground fellowships alike with theological depth and pastoral competence. Enable the Church to meet social needs—literacy, health, vocational training—so that the gospel is confirmed by good works and opens doors in resistant communities. Strengthen ministries to youth and families so new believers have clear discipleship pathways and do not drift away.

Holy Spirit, continue the movement You began: complete the work with perseverance and maturity. I prophesy a Laos where the Church grows not only in number but in spiritual depth—where leaders are equipped, congregations endure, and the gospel becomes a transforming presence across ethnic and geographic divides. Let the harvest be reaped, and the work be finished in Jesus' power.

In Jesus' name, Amen.

113

LATVIA

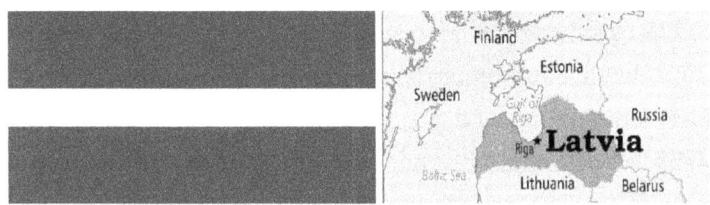

"You will seek me and find me, when you search for me with all your heart."
— Jeremiah 29:13 WEB

Sovereign Searcher of hearts, I stand in the gap for Latvia and declare that a national seeking after God will arise—an honest, whole-hearted pursuit that will not be satisfied with surface religion or secular distraction. I prophesy that the emptiness which prosperity cannot fill will drive many Latvian souls to seek the Lord with intensity, and that in that sincere searching they will meet the living God. Let the moral vacuum left by decades of oppression be filled by a robust hunger for reality, not mere ritual or fad.

Father, send movements of authentic repentance and spiritual curiosity into Riga, Jelgava, and every town where drugs, alcohol, and despair once thrived. Turn what was growth in material comfort into openings for spiritual formation: schools of prayer, public acts of compassion, and gospel conversations among the youth who sense meaninglessness. Empower pastors and Christian leaders to craft compelling discipleship pathways that address loneliness, mental health, and the wounds of the post-Soviet era—programs that combine pastoral care, recovery ministries, and robust teaching rooted in Scripture.

Lord Jesus, bring renewal to families so that homes become places of spiritual nurture rather than mere consumer dwellings. Stir up movements among students, artists, and professionals that model a faith both thoughtful and warm—Christians who can speak credibly into the moral questions of their peers. Multiply ministries that reach those at risk from exploitation and the sex trade, offering restoration, vocational training, and dignity so the most vulnerable have hope and stable futures.

Holy Spirit, breathe a culture of seeking into Latvia: not a superficial curiosity, but a disciplined turning to God that results in visible fruit—reduced suicide, healed families, and communities marked by mercy. I prophesy that the lamp of true faith will shine brighter across the Baltic shores, as many seek and find the Lord with all their heart, and the Kingdom takes hold in streets, schools, and homes.

In Jesus' name, Amen.

114

Lebanon

"Mercy and truth have met together; righteousness and peace have kissed each other."
— Psalm 85:10 WEB

Lord of Compassion and Justice, I lift Lebanon—Beirut and every mountain and valley—before Your throne and declare that mercy and truth will embrace in this fractured land. I prophesy a new season where honest repentance and courageous truth-telling meet tender mercy so that the wounds of decades of war, corruption, and displacement begin to heal. Let righteousness not be an abstract ideal but a working reality that produces tangible peace among Christians, Muslims, refugees, and host communities alike.

Father, pour out supernatural wisdom on leaders who must steward the economy, manage refugee flows, and counter corruption. Give administrators and civic servants uncommon integrity, and provide international partners who act justly and not merely expediently. Release programs that stabilize livelihoods: job creation, fair housing, and education for displaced children—practical mercy that opens hearts to truth and to Christ. Soften hardened attitudes toward refugees and provide channels for their protection and dignified assistance rather than scapegoating.

Lord Jesus, empower the Lebanese Church to be an instrument of reconciliation—hospitable in word and sacrificial in deed. Let congregations pioneer trauma counseling, community centers, and shared projects that unite sects around common good: rebuilding schools, repairing infrastructure, and joint relief clinics. Raise prophetic voices that speak truth to power while offering mercy to the suffering, modeling how righteousness and compassion coexist under Your Lordship.

Holy Spirit, bring locally rooted peace that outlives political cycles: inner healing for war-scarred souls, restored neighborhoods, and courageous civic renewal. I prophesy Lebanon becoming a place where mercy and truth meet, where justice becomes the pathway to peace, and where the Church stands as a witness of God's reconciling power in a weary region.

In Jesus' name, Amen.

115

Lesotho

"For he will deliver the needy when he cries; the poor also, and him that has no helper. He has pity on the poor and needy, and the life of the needy he saves."
— Psalm 72:12–13 WEB

Mighty Defender and Provider, I bring Lesotho before Your throne as an intercessor and declare that You will strengthen the mountain people and save the lives of the needy. I prophesy a strengthening of systems and ministries that deliver water, health care, and opportunity into Maseru and the remote highlands. Where family breakdown, unemployment, and isolation have pressed down, I release divine provision—skills training, community enterprises, and compassionate church networks that restore dignity and sustain life.

Father, bless the mission aviation and radio ministries that already serve isolated settlements. Increase their reach and multiply resources so that medical supplies, teachers, and Bible workers can safely access mountain communities. Provide vocational programs—agricultural innovation, water management, and small-business coaching—that create livelihoods rather than dependence. Equip local leaders to steward these resources with wisdom and transparency so assistance seeds long-term flourishing.

Lord Jesus, we ask for spiritual awakening across Lesotho: that Christian radio and Scripture Union work will translate into changed lives, stronger families, and renewed moral fabric. Raise and train pastors and youth leaders with contextual equipping so they can shepherd isolated congregations effectively. Let schools and youth programs be places of hope where children learn life skills and the gospel, preventing the social drift that fuels substance abuse and despair.

Holy Spirit, bring healing to wounded communities and practical miracles of provision. I prophesy valleys and highlands where the poor receive help, where water flows, where children flourish in school, and where the Church embodies both compassion and truth. Let Lesotho's mountain people experience the Lord's pity and saving power so the nation moves from survival to sustained wholeness.

In Jesus' name, Amen.

116

LIBERIA

"They shall build and inhabit the old waste places; they shall plant vineyards and drink their fruit; they shall also make gardens and eat their fruit."
— Isaiah 61:4 WEB

Restorer King and Hope of Nations, I lift Liberia—Monrovia and all counties—before Your throne and prophesy restoration for what war and trauma have torn down. I declare that the waste places of civil conflict will be rebuilt: towns repaired, families reunited, and communal life renewed. Let returning refugees and those who remained be given work, shelter, and the dignity of contributing to a nation remade in justice and mercy, where the fruit of labors blesses households and communities alike.

Father, provide comprehensive programs for literacy, health, and economic empowerment that address Liberia's low literacy and development challenges. Raise educational initiatives and vocational training tailored to local needs—agriculture, carpentry, health work—so that returning refugees and young Liberians can build livelihoods. Bless public leaders with wisdom to enact reforms that prevent the recurrence of war, ensure fair land distribution, and prioritize reconciliation over revenge.

Lord Jesus, anoint the Church to be central in healing trauma and building social capital. Multiply ministries that offer counseling for survivors, reconciliation programs between former combatants and communities, and church-led clinics and schools that model Kingdom values. Empower Christian leaders to pursue national unity and to champion accountability and transparency so governance no longer replicates old patterns of abuse.

Holy Spirit, move powerfully to transform Liberia into its name: a land of freedom filled with flourishing gardens and stable homes. I prophesy communities rebuilt, orchards and gardens planted, and children growing in schooling and peace—Liberia restored by the God who rebuilds and renews. Let hope become the nation's hallmark and the Church its steady anchor.

In Jesus' name, Amen.

117

LIBYA

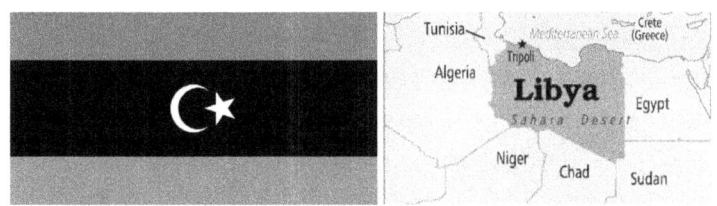

"God is our refuge and strength, a very present help in trouble."
— Psalm 46:1 WEB

Mighty Refuge and Ever-present Help, I lift Libya before Your throne and declare that even amid chaos, the Lord is a shelter for the vulnerable and a source of strength for the weary. I prophesy that neighborhoods in Tripoli, Benghazi, and along desert routes will find pockets of safety where aid reaches the ruined, where migrants and locals alike encounter mercy, and where believers mobilize with courageous compassion. Let the presence of God become tangible amid lawlessness so hearts turn from violence to the Prince of Peace.

Father, protect those who are trafficked, exploited, or stranded on treacherous journeys. Disrupt the engines of human trafficking and provide corridors of rescue and refuge. Raise humanitarian networks—local and international—that operate with wisdom and bravery to deliver food, medical care, and legal protection to migrants and Libyan families affected by conflict. Grant judges and emerging leaders a fear of God and the courage to push for political settlement that secures civic life.

Lord Jesus, empower underground and visible Christian ministries to be beacons of hope: safe houses that receive believers and seekers, medical teams that heal wounds, and translators who bring Scripture and compassionate counsel. Strengthen believers who risk persecution to serve; give them protection, practical resources, and strategic partnerships so ministry can continue even in fragile security conditions. Let the gospel find fertile ground among migrants and locals overwhelmed by loss and longing.

Holy Spirit, bring a tide of rescue and reconciliation across Libya: political openings for stable governance, practical rebuilding of infrastructure, and spiritual breakthroughs where many find salvation in desperation. I prophesy that Libya's deserts will see pathways of compassion and that cities will know restoration; let the Lord be the refuge and strength that leads this nation into a season of healing.

In Jesus' name, Amen.

118

LIECHTENSTEIN

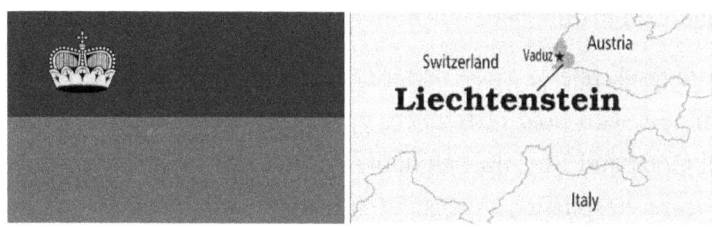

"Be still, and know that I am God; I will be exalted among the nations, I will be exalted in the earth."
— Psalm 46:10 WEB

Sovereign Lord, King above every principality, I come before You as a bold intercessor for Liechtenstein and I declare that Your quiet, sovereign reign will interrupt the noise of nominalism and cultural drift. I prophesy a season in which Your calm presence displaces restless religion and the seeking after worldly status. Let the prince's halls, the parish pews, and the quiet valleys of Vaduz become places where people cease striving and acknowledge Your supreme lordship; may Your exaltation ripple through families and civic life so that reverence for You replaces indifferent ritual.

Father, by Your Spirit renew theological hunger across this small principality. Where faith has become a polite cultural identity more than an embodied devotion, breathe repentance and curiosity so that people again learn to wait on You, to listen, and to be led by Scripture. Strengthen the small evangelical fellowship with vision and depth, and bless the Catholic charismatic threads among the royal family with humility and truth so that influence is exercised in mercy. Equip pastors and lay leaders to cultivate reflective discipleship—small groups, careful Bible teaching, and mentoring that form mature believers rather than mere church-goers.

Lord Jesus, release a new pattern of worship that combines reverent stillness with bold obedience. Let the growing numbers of non-religious and Muslim neighbors be met not by polemics but by sincere hospitality, consistent integrity, and winsome witness. Raise up families and workplace believers who live exemplary Christian ethics—financial honesty, care for the vulnerable, and sacrificial generosity—so that Luxembourgish-style prosperity does not become Liechtenstein's idol but a platform for gospel stewardship.

Holy Spirit, bring a gentle reformation: hearts softened, minds renewed, and a populace who knows that God is God. I prophesy Liechtenstein becoming a place where stillness is spiritual strength, where the Prince's household and ordinary citizens alike know the Lord intimately, and where the nation's high human development is matched by deep, renewing faith. May Your name alone be exalted here.

In Jesus' name, Amen.

119

LITHUANIA

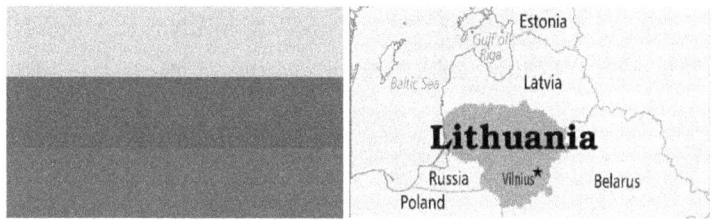

"Put on therefore, as God's chosen ones, holy and beloved, tender mercies, kindness, humbleness of mind, meekness, longsuffering; forbearing one another and forgiving one another, if anyone has a complaint against another; even as Christ forgave you, so you also do. And above all these things put on love, which is the bond of perfection."
— Colossians 3:12–14 WEB

Merciful Father and Restorer of broken societies, I stand in the gap for Lithuania and declare that the Lord will clothe this nation in the garments of Christlike character—compassion, humility, forgiveness and steadfast love. I prophesy a moral and spiritual springtime that addresses the moral vacuum left by decades of oppression and sudden freedom. Where substance abuse, human trafficking, and the pain of family breakdown laid waste to lives, let tender mercy and restored community become the new cultural clothing of the people.

Father, stir the Church to embody practical kindness that heals social wounds. Train pastors, social workers, and volunteers to run after the marginalized—those battling addiction, young women at risk of trafficking, and men tempted by despondency. Let counseling centers, recovery houses, and safe-haven programs multiply. Give government leaders godly humility to enact policies that protect the vulnerable, invest in family supports, and restore vocational opportunities so youth do not fall back into despair by default.

Lord Jesus, pour out long-suffering patience on those who minister to communities traumatized by history and modern pressures. Teach congregations to bear one another's burdens with steadfastness, to forgive old wounds, and to lead reconciliation initiatives in towns that still nurse resentments. Let Christian schools, radio, and local ministries model ethical living and robust discipleship so that spiritual transformation accompanies economic progress; show Lithuania how to grow in prosperity without losing the soul of the nation.

Holy Spirit, bind Lithuania together with the perfect bond of love. I prophesy neighborhoods reformed by care, workplaces led by conscience, and families renewed by grace—so that the Church's compassion becomes the engine of social renewal and a light to Europe. May Christlike virtue shape the nation's future.

In Jesus' name, Amen.

120

LUXEMBOURG

> "But sanctify the Lord God in your hearts: and always be ready to give an answer to everyone who asks you a reason for the hope that is in you, with meekness and fear."
> — 1 Peter 3:15 WEB

Lord of every tongue and people, I bring Luxembourg before Your throne and declare that the cosmopolitan crossroads of Europa will become a wellspring of humble, winsome witness. I prophesy that Christians—local and expatriate—will be sanctified in heart and quickened to speak the hope within them wherever opportunity appears: in banks, embassies, international schools, and marketplaces. Let believers learn to give reasoned, gentle testimony that honors both truth and cultural sensitivity, so the gospel finds attentive ears in this religiously diverse nation.

Father, mobilize expatriate congregations and native churches to cooperate strategically for outreach among the many faiths and nationalities present. Provide language training, culturally relevant apologetics, and hospitality networks that welcome newcomers and open doors for gospel conversation. Raise lay evangelists who work in government, finance, NGOs and the arts—people who can model Christian virtues in public life and answer questions with both intellect and love.

Lord Jesus, equip churches to disciple believers in how to live out the gospel among pluralistic peers without compromise. Encourage church planting among immigrant communities while strengthening local congregations to be centers of integration and mercy ministries—English classes, legal help, and community events that demonstrate Christ's love practically. Bless theological training that balances doctrinal clarity with cultural wisdom so Luxembourg's faith communities can be both faithful and effective.

Holy Spirit, loosen hearts across the Grand Duchy to hear and receive the reasoned hope of Christ. I prophesy an outpouring of humble apologetic witness that draws many from different backgrounds into relationship with Jesus—so this small nation becomes a hub not only of global finance, but of faithful, winsome testimony and transforming love.

In Jesus' name, Amen.

121

MACAU

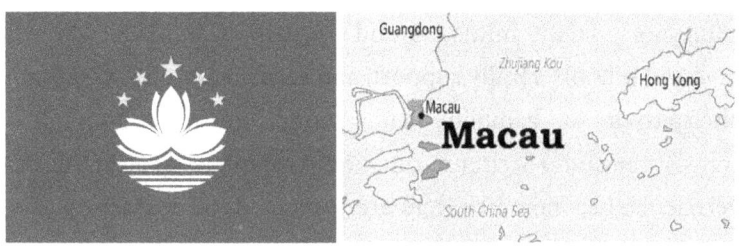

"Arise, shine; for your light has come, and the glory of Yahweh has risen upon you."
— Isaiah 60:1 WEB

Glorious God, Light of the nations and Restorer of ancient witness, I come before You for Macau and boldly announce that Your light will arise over this city of casinos and diaspora. I prophesy the dawning of a spiritual breakthrough that reclaims Macau's historic Christian heritage: churches renewed, missionaries emboldened, and local believers awakened to the urgent call to shine where darkness and superstition have held sway. Let the memory of Macau's early witness be the seedbed for a new harvest.

Father, empower pastors and leaders to plant vibrant congregations that resist turnover and shallow spirituality. Replace transient ministry patterns with long-term, contextual strategies: sustained discipleship in Cantonese and Portuguese, stable pastoral leadership, and robust training for lay evangelists who understand local rhythms. Where fear of the local god "A-Ma" and occult influence intimidates, let the gospel's power and testimonies of changed lives break the hold of superstition.

Lord Jesus, send workers who love the city—evangelists, counselors, youth ministers and business Christians who will invest in schools, family support, and media that offer wholesome alternatives to gambling and moral drift. Multiply Bible translation, audio Scripture, and discipleship materials in the local vernaculars so new believers are grounded. Strengthen existing congregations to be visible centers of care—helping migrants, supporting families, and offering recovery from addictions spawned by the tourism economy.

Holy Spirit, cause Macau to arise and shine: restore its pioneering missionary identity so that the city becomes once again a gateway for the gospel into mainland China and southeast Asia. I prophesy churches that outlast the turnover, a swelling of sincere conversions, and a community where the glory of the Lord replaces fear and empty leisure with faithful worship and life-giving witness. Let Macau's light blaze for Your Name.

In Jesus' name, Amen.

122

MADAGASCAR

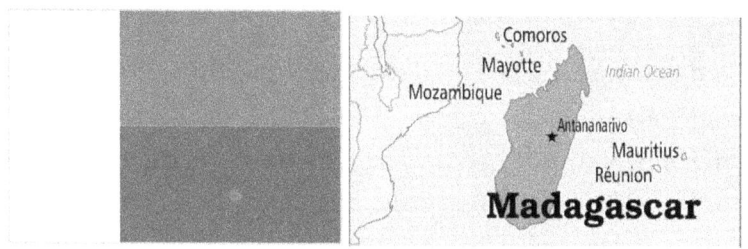

"But the fruit of the Spirit is love, joy, peace, longsuffering, kindness, goodness, faithfulness, gentleness, self-control: against such there is no law."
— Galatians 5:22–23 WEB

Holy and Living God, Source of every good fruit, I lift Madagascar before Your throne and declare that the worn vines of nominal faith will begin to bear true spiritual fruit. I prophesy a fresh work of the Spirit across Antananarivo and every province—where ancestral veneration and syncretism have blurred the gospel, the Spirit will bring clear conversion marked by love, joy, peace and a visible transformation in conduct. Let churches awake from spiritual sleep to be communities that demonstrate the fruit of the Spirit in public and private life.

Father, send revival that pairs true repentance with intensive biblical teaching so that Christians move from outward ritual into inward reality. Empower pastors and seminary teachers with renewed zeal and deep doctrinal clarity; equip them to confront witchcraft and ancestral fear with compassion and deliverance grounded in Scripture. Multiply discipleship structures—home groups, children's training, and leadership pipelines—so new believers are formed, not just counted.

Lord Jesus, strengthen ministries that display God's goodness practically—healing clinics, agricultural initiatives, literacy programs, and family counseling—that win credibility and open hearts to the gospel. Bless radio and Scripture audio campaigns that penetrate rural areas where illiteracy and old practices persist. Raise indigenous evangelists who understand Malagasy culture and can translate the gospel away from syncretism into living faith, producing visible fruit in families and communities.

Holy Spirit, bring patient endurance and self-control so communities move past the veneer of faith into lasting righteousness. I prophesy Madagascar revived: churches filled with gentle, faithful believers; communities showing kindness and justice; and a nation where the fruit of the Spirit becomes the hallmark of Christian witness—drawing many into true faith and releasing lasting transformation.

In Jesus' name, Amen.

123

MALAWI

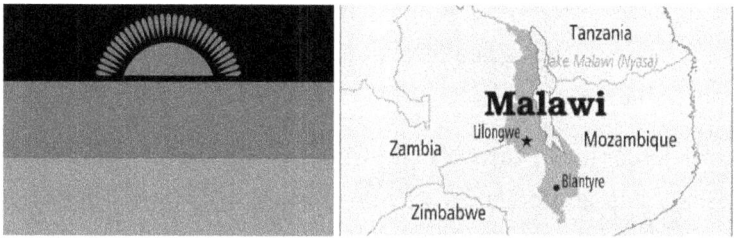

"Seek the welfare of the city where I have sent you into exile, and pray to Yahweh for it; for in its welfare you will have welfare."
— Jeremiah 29:7 WEB

Sovereign Lord, Wise Planner and Shepherd of nations, I stand in the gap for Malawi and declare that I will seek the welfare of Lilongwe and every rural village as if it were my own. I call down your wisdom into the halls of leadership and into the hearts of mothers and fathers who till soil and teach children. I prophesy that prayer and policy will be yoked together: leaders who pray and planners who act with humility, foresight, and long-term biblical wisdom. I claim, in faith, that the nation's flourishing will be the measure we pursue—not short-term gain, but sustainable stewardship that blesses future generations.

Father, I ask You to make governors, ministers, and community elders prudent stewards of scarce resources. Turn the grip of poverty into strategies for agricultural renewal, land care, and education so that increasing population pressure does not crush the land or the people. Let schools be strengthened, literacy rise beyond today's limits, and health initiatives—especially AIDS prevention—become culturally effective. Release godly advisers to your leaders who will design family-centered social programs, water projects and agricultural training that honor the Creator and benefit the poor.

Lord Jesus, move through the Church with a renewed zeal for discipleship and practical service. I pray that Christian influence will be manifested not as dominion but as humble service—churches that run literacy classes, clinics, and micro-enterprise programs; pastors who are disciples and disciples who make disciples. Protect the young from despair; cultivate vocational training that keeps talent at home rather than sending it away. Strengthen the evangelical impulse to plant homes of faith in villages and cities alike, so that spiritual formation accompanies social development.

Holy Spirit, empower Malawian believers with endurance, compassion, and clarity. Let prayer networks arise across denominations, binding the Church to the nation's welfare. I prophesy Malawi will become a model of integrated ministry and policy—leaders acting with wisdom, families sustained, and communities flourishing as the Lord's provision and people's wise stewardship meet. May Thy Kingdom come in Lilongwe, the lakeshore, and the highlands.

In Jesus' name, Amen.

124

MALAYSIA

"Do not be conformed to this world, but be transformed by the renewing of your mind, that you may prove what is that good and acceptable and perfect will of God."
— Romans 12:2 WEB

Mighty Redeemer and Ruler of hearts, I come before You for Malaysia and declare transformation over Kuala Lumpur, over towns and kampongs, and over the many peoples who live under one crown and many traditions. I ask that Christians and leaders alike resist mere cultural conformity—whether to ethnic nationalism, political expediency, or the seductions of material comfort—and instead be shaped by minds renewed in Christ. I prophesy a spiritually discerning Church that can prove God's good, acceptable, and perfect will for the nation in every sphere of life.

Father, raise leaders who govern with wisdom that honors all communities—moderate and conservative Muslims, ethnic minorities, Orang Asli, and immigrant neighbours. Give statesmen the courage to enact policies that protect human dignity and the freedom to follow conscience while preserving national cohesion. Break corrupt systems that have enriched the few; replace favoritism with justice and balanced development. Let the Malay heart be heard and respected while creating space for minority flourishing and evangelistic compassion.

Lord Jesus, strengthen the Malaysian Church to reach the least-reached Malay communities with humility and cultural sensitivity. Equip house churches and multi-ethnic fellowships to disciple new believers deeply so conversions are not merely cultural shifts but rooted transformations. Provide boldness and prudence for outreach where public worship is constrained; multiply contextual training for leaders who can shepherd Malay-background believers safely and sensitively. Bless ministries to the Orang Asli and other animist groups with literacy, Scripture in local tongues, and practical care that opens hearts to the gospel.

Holy Spirit, renew minds across the archipelago that are captive to fear, pride, or tribalism—bring humility, repentance, and vision for multi-ethnic unity under Christ. I prophesy Malaysia will not be defined only by political labels but by a maturing witness: a Church that is courageous, compassionate, and wise, drawing many into the Kingdom and proving God's will for the whole nation.

In Jesus' name, Amen.

125

Maldives

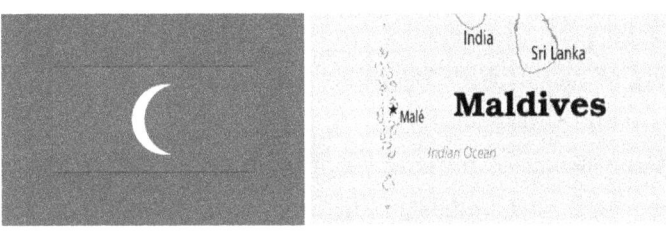

"The light shines in the darkness; and the darkness didn't comprehend it."
— John 1:5 WEB

Lord of light and hidden mercies, I lift the Maldives before Your throne and declare that Your light will pierce the shadows that cover these islands. I prophesy a breaking of strongholds—of occult practice, teen drug despair, prideful pleasure-seeking, and enforced religious uniformity—by the steady, penetrating radiance of Christ. Even where darkness has been thick and public expression of faith forbidden, I speak hope into private hearts: the gospel's light will shine in hidden places, bringing rescue and new life.

Father, protect and embolden those who are lonely, abused, or trapped in cycles of addiction. Provide covert but effective pathways for counseling, recovery programs, and vocational training that restore dignity to teens and young adults. Soften the hearts of families and community leaders toward care rather than condemnation. Open avenues—digital, relational, and discreet—for Maldivians to encounter Scripture and testimonies of transformation without risking lives.

Lord Jesus, raise a hidden, faithful witness among expatriates and discreet local believers who will embody gospel love through acts of mercy—healthcare, education, and trauma support. Let the beauty of sacrificial service draw curious hearts to question the idols of pleasure and fear. Break the grip of fanditha and occult fear with the power of testimonies: lives transformed, relationships healed, and communities finding new hope in You.

Holy Spirit, shine in the darkness of Maldivian islands—so fear is replaced by courage, addiction by restoration, and isolation by community. I prophesy that the hidden light will become a beacon: private faith strengthened, rescued lives multiplied, and a people quietly awakened to the living Christ even under restriction. Let Thy Kingdom come across Atolls and coral shores.

In Jesus' name, Amen.

126

MALI

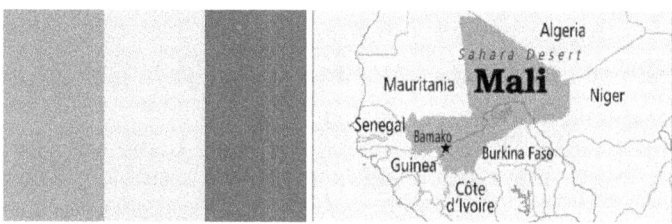

"Give the king your judgments, O God, and your righteousness to the king's son. He will judge your people with righteousness, and your poor with justice. He will deliver the needy when he cries; the poor also, and him who has no helper. He will spare the poor and needy, and he will save the souls of the needy."
— Psalm 72:1,4,12–14 WEB

Sovereign Judge and Protector of the afflicted, I present Mali before Your throne and plead for rulers who will rule with righteousness and compassion. I declare that those in authority—current and those You will raise—will give priority to justice for the poor, protection for the displaced, and rescue for the vulnerable. Where coups, jihadist violence and ethnic conflict have ravaged towns and villages, I prophesy a turnaround: leaders who value human life and create systems that deliver food, medicine, and security to desperate families.

Father, grant wisdom and courage to security forces and civic leaders so they can restrain extremist groups and criminal militias without unjustly harming civilians. Open paths for reconciliation between herders and farmers, and bless initiatives that provide alternative livelihoods to defuse the resource-driven conflicts. Send foreign and internal investment that avoids exploitation, focuses on sustainable agriculture, and equips health systems to reverse child mortality and malnutrition.

Lord Jesus, commission Your Church to be a visible presence of mercy—churches that feed the hungry, clinics that heal the wounded, and schools that teach hope. Strengthen believers who remain in the north and south with courage to serve amid danger. Multiply medical outreaches, trauma counseling, and community reconciliation projects that heal deep wounds. Use Christian ministries to bring relief to displaced people and to teach practical farming techniques that resist desertification.

Holy Spirit, deliver Mali from cycles of violence and make the nation a place where the needy are seen, helped, and restored. I prophesy that the poor will find advocates, children will live to adulthood, and communities will move from fear to flourishing. Let justice roll, let compassion lead, and let the light of Christ shine in Bamako and beyond.

In Jesus' name, Amen.

127

Malta

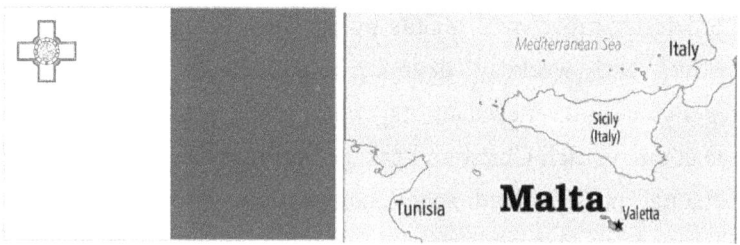

"That Christ may dwell in your hearts through faith; that you, being rooted and grounded in love, may be able to comprehend with all the saints what is the breadth, length, depth and height; and to know the love of Christ, which passes knowledge; that you may be filled with all the fullness of God."
— Ephesians 3:17–19 WEB

Sovereign Lord and Ancient Rock, I lift Malta—the island first warmed by apostolic presence—before Your throne and declare that the historic fidelity of tradition will turn into a living, personal knowledge of Christ. I prophesy an awakening where attendance does not remain ritual alone but becomes the soil for hearts to be rooted deeply in the love that surpasses knowledge. Let Maltese identity as a Christian people mature into a people who personally know and walk with Jesus.

Father, renew clergy and catechists with pastoral passion so liturgy becomes encounter and sacraments become life-change. Give pastors humility to preach not only rite but relationship; equip small groups and house fellowships where believers wrestle honestly with faith, confession, morale, and discipleship. Let schools and family ministries teach children the reality of a living Savior, not merely cultural customs.

Lord Jesus, move over Malta's public life—bring authenticity to festival and weekday devotion alike. Bless movements of repentance and renewal among youth, families, and elders so that the country's rich Christian heritage becomes a launching pad for personal holiness and social compassion. Encourage Maltese Christians to lead with charity in public policy, hospitality, and mercy ministries to the refugee and the lonely, displaying the love that anchors faith.

Holy Spirit, make Malta a place where Christ truly dwells in hearts: rooted in love, filled with God's fullness, and outwardly generous in action. I prophesy a renewed Malta that carries apostolic legacy into a powerful present testimony—churches alive, families transformed, and a nation saturated with the love of Christ.

In Jesus' name, Amen.

128

MARSHALL ISLANDS

"Fear not, for I am with you; be not dismayed, for I am your God. I will strengthen you; yes, I will help you; yes, I will uphold you with the right hand of my righteousness."
— Isaiah 41:10 WEB

Sovereign God, Rock and Refuge of island peoples, I come before You as a prophetic intercessor for the Marshall Islands and declare that fear will be displaced and Your sustaining presence will shape this nation's future. I stand in the gap for Majuro and every atoll, lifting up those who carry the scars of occupation, nuclear testing, and intergenerational trauma. I prophesy Your strengthening hand over families and leaders—so that weakness becomes strength, despair becomes hope, and dependence on external, destructive patterns gives way to resilient, godly stewardship of land, health and culture.

Father, breathe wisdom into the rulers and community elders who make decisions about economic dependency and cultural preservation. Raise leaders with moral courage to demand fair reparations, to resist harmful external pressures, and to steward natural resources and international aid with integrity. Grant policymakers vision to transition from dependency toward diversified, sustainable economies that honor traditional land rights and restore dignity to communities. Let national strategies include long-term health monitoring, genetic care, and cancer treatment programs so physical wounds receive sustained attention alongside spiritual healing.

Lord Jesus, heal the social fabric torn by past exploitation. Restore the value of Marshallese traditions—family, land, and communal identity—as God-honoring goods rather than things to be discarded. Empower the Church to be a central agent of restoration: counseling for trauma, ministries for the sick, education for the young, and cultural renewal projects that transmit wisdom and identity. Raise prayerful activists who are also peacemakers, bridging younger and older generations, and equipping the people to narrate a hopeful future rooted in truth and grace.

Holy Spirit, uphold the afflicted and a people who have suffered injustices—hold them up with righteousness, give them strength beyond their resources, and steady their hearts for long work of restoration. I prophesy a Marshall Islands that rises from the shadows of testing into a season of healing, self-governance, and spiritual revival—where the islanders steward their heritage with dignity and the light of Christ shapes every plan.

In Jesus' name, Amen.

129

MARTINIQUE

 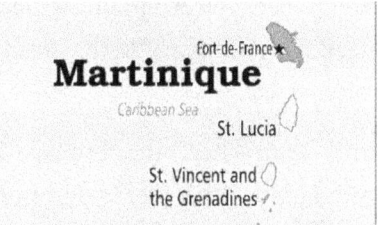

"Therefore, since we are surrounded by so great a cloud of witnesses, let us also lay aside every weight, and the sin which so easily entangles us, and let us run with endurance the race that is set before us; looking to Jesus the author and finisher of our faith."
— Hebrews 12:1–2 WEB

Lord Jesus, Captain of my salvation, I come as a passionate intercessor for Martinique and declare that your people will cast off the chains of past hurts, addictions, and fractured families and will run the Christian race with renewed endurance and vision. I prophesy that churches across Fort-de-France and the islands will grow deeper in discipleship, producing leaders who persevere through trials and who shepherd wounded youth into mature service. Let the legacy of survivors become a testimony that births gospel perseverance and faithful ministries.

Father, breathe revival into the evangelical presence—Assemblies of God, Baptists, Nazarenes and others—so they move from good intention to sustainable impact. Equip pastors with practical pastoral care training, addiction ministry tools, and outreach methodologies that reach the many young people coming from dysfunctional backgrounds. Multiply internship and call-discovery programs that invite youth into full-time service, providing mentorship, theological training, and opportunities for meaningful ministry so that a generation is not merely helped but empowered.

Lord Jesus, heal the broken families and replace cycles of immorality with patterns of restoration and holiness. Let churches be known for effective recovery ministries: safe houses, counseling networks, vocational training, and family reconciliation programs that restore dignity and provide pathways out of illicit lifestyle. Bless local Christian schools and community initiatives that care for children and teens, offering alternatives to drug culture and the lure of exploitation.

Holy Spirit, sustain Martinique's believers with patient endurance and joyful hope; cause congregations to become centers of healing and training. I prophesy a surge of faithful servants raised up from among the healed—people whose stories of rescue will become the banner for a wider revival, and whose endurance will inspire island-wide transformation in family life, morality, and ministry.

In Jesus' name, Amen.

130

MAURITANIA

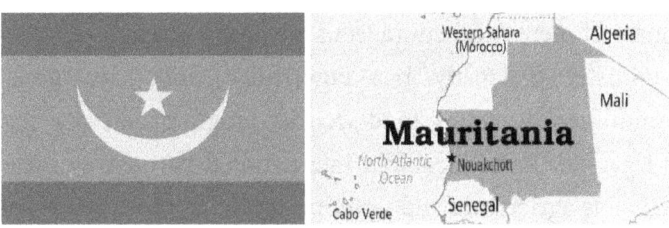

> "But let justice roll on like waters, and righteousness like an overflowing stream."
> — Amos 5:24 WEB

Righteous Judge and Avenger of the Oppressed, I come before You for Mauritania and declare that justice and righteousness will begin to flow across Nouakchott and the desert towns like living water. I prophesy an end to hidden slavery, the exposure of traffickers and exploiters, and the rise of systems that protect the poor, the illiterate, and the food-insecure. Let the nations' leaders and civil servants be stirred by conscience and courage to enact reforms that rescue the vulnerable and bring equitable access to land and livelihood.

Father, pour wisdom into government and NGO leaders as they manage scarce arable land, looming desertification, and possible oil wealth. Grant safeguards to ensure that any resource discovery benefits the many rather than a corrupt few. Provide transparent governance structures, anti-corruption mechanisms, and robust social programs that confront malnutrition and illiteracy. Rescue those trapped in slavery-like conditions: legislate uncompromising laws, enforce them with integrity, and fund rehabilitation for freed persons.

Lord Jesus, move the Church—however small and hidden—to be a source of mercy and courageous advocacy. Strengthen believers to minister discreetly but powerfully among marginalized communities, providing food security programs, literacy classes, and legal aid. Raise local and international partners to invest in sustainable agriculture and water projects that resist desert spread and rebuild communities. Empower grassroots movements that defend women and children against exploitation and champion family restoration.

Holy Spirit, break the strongholds of fear, greed, and cultural complicity with injustice. I prophesy a Mauritania transformed by justice: freed captives walking in dignity, schools reaching the illiterate, food flowing to the hungry, and courts prosecuting the wicked. Let righteousness overflow like a river across this land, and let the Name of Jesus be associated with liberation and hope.

In Jesus' name, Amen.

131

MAURITIUS

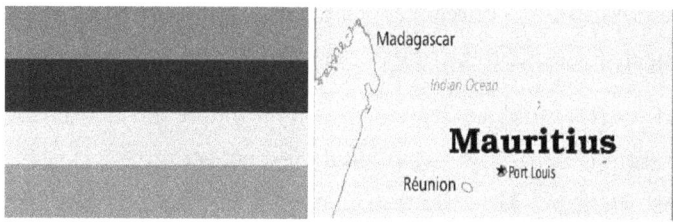

"But you will receive power when the Holy Spirit has come upon you; and you will be witnesses to me in Jerusalem, and in all Judea and Samaria, and to the end of the earth."
— Acts 1:8 WEB

Lord of the Harvest and Giver of Power, I lift Mauritius to Your throne and declare that the island's rich multicultural soil will birth bold, Spirit-filled witness. I prophesy that Christians across Port Louis and the islands will be empowered to cross ethnic and religious lines with love, cultural sensitivity and prophetic boldness—reaching Hindus, Muslims, and those bound by ancestral ties with the transforming gospel. Let the Church receive fresh power for witness and multiplied fruit even in hard-to-reach communities.

Father, grant the Church discernment to engage wisely in a society shaped by Hinduization and entrenched ethnic identity. Raise a generation of leaders who understand local cultures and speak into them with humility and strategic compassion. Bless multi-ethnic fellowships, equip inter-denominational networks, and fund contextual ministries that deploy Scripture and gospel witness in indigenous languages and idioms. Provide targeted outreach to the Orang Asli and to unreached island communities with contextual evangelism and compassionate service.

Lord Jesus, embolden your people to combine truth with love—presenting Christ in ways that respect culture yet call for transformation. Multiply testimonies of Hindus coming to Jesus through the visible kindness and integrity of Christians. Strengthen discipleship pathways so converts are not isolated but grounded in community and doctrine. Encourage churches to partner with social ministries—education, healthcare, and vocational training—that demonstrate the gospel in tangible ways and open hearts to the message.

Holy Spirit, pour out boldness and contextual wisdom across Mauritius; let the islands be a gospel laboratory where multi-ethnic, Spirit-empowered growth becomes the norm. I prophesy a Church that reflects the beauty of God's Kingdom—varied in culture but united in Christ—so Mauritius becomes a place where the nations are reached and disciples multiply to the ends of the earth.

In Jesus' name, Amen.

132

MAYOTTE

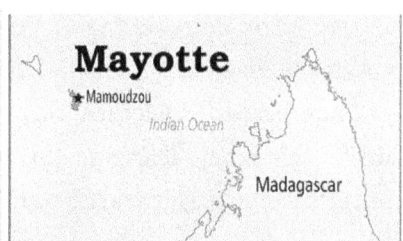

"Blessed are the poor in spirit, for theirs is the kingdom of heaven."
— Matthew 5:3 WEB

King Jesus, Merciful King of the poor and humbled, I present Mayotte before You and declare that the spiritual poverty that has kept its people bound will become fertile soil for the Kingdom. I prophesy that where Maore Islam is entangled with spirit possession and complacency, the gentle power of Christ will awaken a hunger for true life. Let the islands—named for death—be transformed into places of living hope, where the humble receive the Kingdom and communities begin to witness real spiritual renewal.

Father, break the complacency that economic assistance has fostered; breathe a holy discontent that moves people from comfort to compassion and from acquiescence to spiritual seeking. Raise local believers and visiting workers who live incarnationally—ministering openly in permitted contexts, yet wisely, offering mercy ministries that meet real needs: clean water, schooling, healthcare, and family support that show the love of Christ in action.

Lord Jesus, intervene against the stronghold of magic and spirit possession by empowering testimony-centered evangelism and prayerful deliverance ministries that are culturally sensitive and Scripture-based. Strengthen the Assemblies of God and other faithful churches engaging in open-air evangelism; protect converts from social backlash and provide discipleship that leads to enduring faith. Multiply small groups and house fellowships that can support new believers and form lasting spiritual communities.

Holy Spirit, kindle a revival in Mayotte: bring conviction and humility, mobilize prayer for the islands, and grant the people a courageous break from old patterns. I prophesy that Mayotte will live up to a new name—a place of spiritual life—where the poor in spirit are comforted, the oppressed find liberty, and the gospel flourishes in both word and deed.

In Jesus' name, Amen.

133

Mexico

> "Blessed is the nation whose God is the LORD; and the people he has chosen for his own inheritance."
> — Psalm 33:12 WEB

Sovereign God and King of righteousness, I stand in holy intercession over Mexico and declare Your blessing to rest upon this great nation when You are enthroned as Lord in the hearts of its people. I speak a prophetic reversal over lands riven by cartels, extortion, and the business of death: let the rule of law be strengthened, let corrupt trade be exposed, and let the Church rise as a powerful moral influence in cities and pueblos. I call heaven's intervention into the places where violence, trafficking and the economy of sin have taken root — that when Your Lordship is acknowledged, blessing will follow in streets, homes, and markets.

Father, pour wisdom into judges, police, and legislators so that justice is no longer perverted by bribes or terror but functions to protect the weak. Grant leaders courage to confront the cartel networks that profit from drug demand abroad and exploitation at home. Raise up principled prosecutors and honest public servants who will dismantle the economic and political structures that allow trafficking, kidnapping, and extortion to flourish. Let social policy prioritize victims and create robust rehabilitation and prevention systems that address root causes: poverty, broken families, and lack of opportunity.

Lord Jesus, breathe revival into the Catholic and evangelical heart of Mexico so that cultural religion gives way to living discipleship. Strengthen discipleship in every congregation—Catholic and Protestant—so converts are formed, not merely counted. Multiply pastors willing to serve in the poorest barrios and rural villages; send teams to the slums and to those displaced by violence with gospel compassion, trauma counseling, and tangible help. Enable churches to be centers of restoration—providing education, mentoring, and vocational pathways that offer honest alternatives to cartel life.

Holy Spirit, convict a generation of Mexicans to reject the idols of quick gain and ancestral spiritism and to embrace the Lordship of Christ. I prophesy communities healed from fear, families restored, and neighborhoods reclaimed by gospel light—so Mexico becomes a place where the people truly live under the blessing of the Lord.

In Jesus' name, Amen.

134

Moldova

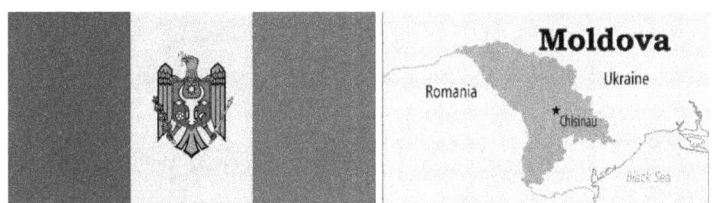

"Learn to do right; seek justice. Rescue the oppressed, defend the fatherless, plead for the widow."
— Isaiah 1:17 WEB

Righteous Judge and Defender of the weak, I come as an intercessor for Moldova and declare that Your justice will begin to heal Chişinău, Transnistria, and the countryside. I lift up the victims of trafficking, the women deceived abroad, and the families broken by economic exile. Let the Church and the state be united in a holy determination to rescue the oppressed, protect the fatherless, and speak for those who cannot speak for themselves. Move in power to dismantle criminal rings and the shadow economies that profit from human misery.

Father, grant boldness and integrity to law enforcement so that smuggling networks in Transnistria are exposed and disempowered. Strengthen reform-minded officials to pursue economic policies that create meaningful work at home, reducing the desperate outflow of labor. Provide training and resourcing for border control that respects human dignity while cutting the lifelines of traffickers. Raise vocational programs and small-business initiatives that allow young men and women to stay and build lives rather than sell their futures.

Lord Jesus, empower the Church to be a refuge and a training ground: shelters for returning victims, counseling for trauma, and literacy and job-skills programs that restore dignity. Multiply pastors and social workers who can reach the slums and villages with both truth and mercy, giving practical pathways out of addiction and abuse. Bless cross-border partnerships that stand against exploitation, and enable national networks to lobby for better protections and prosecutions.

Holy Spirit, awaken Moldova to a vision of justice rooted in compassion. I prophesy a nation where the widow and orphan are defended, where organized crime loses its grip, and where God's people are known for rescuing the vulnerable and building a future of hope. Let righteousness take root and peace follow.

In Jesus' name, Amen.

135

Monaco

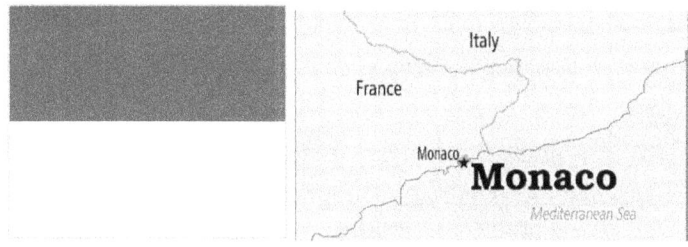

"But seek first the kingdom of God and his righteousness; and all these things will be given to you as well."
— Matthew 6:33 WEB

King of kings, Lover of souls and Lord over wealth, I intercede for Monaco and declare that in the midst of luxury and abundance the Father's kingdom will be sought first. I prophesy that the tiny principality by the sea will become a place where spiritual longing is met by simple, faithful witness—where expatriates and the wealthy are confronted not by condemnation but by the gentle clarity of the gospel. Let believers here put the priority of God's reign above self-indulgence, and may public life be shaped by righteousness rather than merely privilege.

Father, awaken the small body of evangelical believers and the faithful in historic denominations to strategic, compassionate outreach. Give Monaco's Christian fellowship boldness to host hospitable gatherings, intellectual engagements, and discreet acts of mercy that pierce the heart of a culture enamored with luxury. Provide creative ministries that reach expats—business networks, English-language Bible studies, and service projects that attract those who long for meaning beyond material success.

Lord Jesus, raise up faithful leaders from among the scattered churches—monégasque, Anglican, Catholic and evangelical—who will embody righteousness and compassion in public life. Let Christian families and professionals become exemplars of integrity, generosity, and humility, creating a moral influence disproportionate to their small numbers. Bless initiatives that serve the poor and isolated in the community, hospitality to newcomers, and spiritual formation for those seeking depth.

Holy Spirit, stir deep hunger in the hearts of Monaco's residents for the reality the world cannot buy. I prophesy that the principality will not only glitter with wealth but glow with godly witness: a community where the kingdom is sought, righteousness is prized, and lives are transformed by the presence of Christ.

In Jesus' name, Amen.

136

Mongolia

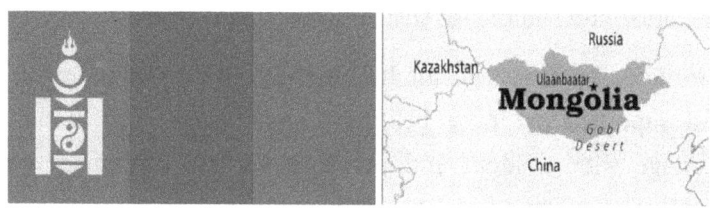

"Behold, I will do a new thing; now it will spring forth; will you not be aware of it? I will even make a way in the wilderness, and rivers in the desert."
— Isaiah 43:19 WEB

Lord of new beginnings, I lift Mongolia—Ulaanbaatar, the steppes and mountain towns—before Your throne and declare that You are already doing a new thing among the Mongolian peoples. I prophesy that the remarkable growth of the Church will deepen into maturity and fruitfulness: indigenous expressions of worship multiplied, churches rooted in Scripture and culture, and fresh rivers of compassion and mission carving life through spiritual deserts. Let the momentum of past decades be the launching pad for enduring movement that sends laborers outward as well as inward.

Father, strengthen the young Mongolian Church with theological depth and pastoral maturity. Provide seminaries, mentoring networks, and contextual training that elevate leaders who understand nomadic heart and urban challenge alike. Empower missionaries from Mongolia to reach unreached tribes and neighbouring peoples, and give the Church logistical support—literature in Mongolian, radio, and practical ministries that address education and health—to sustain widespread growth.

Lord Jesus, protect the Church from the twin dangers of imitation and superficiality; raise believers who engage their Buddhist heritage with wisdom and proclaim Christ's supremacy with humility. Let churches be centers of social transformation—schools, clinics, and youth programs that win trust and demonstrate the gospel's power to change families and communities. Bless worship styles that are authentically Mongolian and yet thoroughly biblical, drawing many into genuine conversion and discipleship.

Holy Spirit, continue to do what only You can do: make a way where there was none, nourish desert places with living water, and birth movements of faith that transform cities and steppes alike. I prophesy Mongolian Christians maturing into a sending people—rooted, bold, and fruitful—so that the new thing You began grows into a lasting, nation-shaping revival.

In Jesus' name, Amen.

137

MONTENEGRO

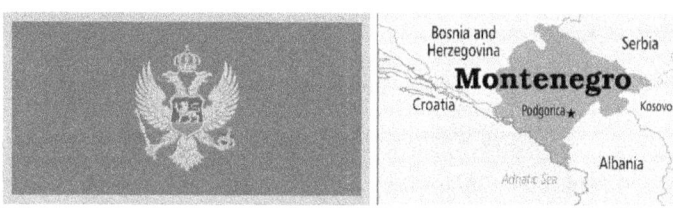

"If possible, so far as it depends on you, be at peace with all people."
— Romans 12:18 WEB

Prince of Peace and Healer of ancient wounds, I stand in prayer over Montenegro and declare peace into Podgorica, coastal towns, and highland villages. I prophesy that ethno-religious tensions will be softened by repentance, humility, and a new hunger for the unity that Christ brings. Let leaders and citizens alike work toward reconciliation, resist the poison of historical hatred, and pursue justice and equity so that every community—Serb, Montenegrin, Albanian, Bosniak—can flourish without fear.

Father, bless the government with integrity and the will to root out corruption that divides society. Raise fair judges and transparent institutions that model accountability and protect minority rights. Enable civic initiatives that bring communities together—shared schools, cultural exchanges, joint service projects—so ordinary people build relationships that outlast political rhetoric.

Lord Jesus, raise peacemakers among clergy, youth leaders and lay activists who will teach forgiveness and practical reconciliation. Empower churches to lead in restorative practices: community dialogues, joint humanitarian efforts, and public acts of reconciliation that show hearts changed by grace. Let the gospel be the bridge that persuades people to choose truth over tribalism and compassion over revenge.

Holy Spirit, sustain Montenegro in a season of nation-building that values justice and harmony. I prophesy a land where ethnic harmony is not merely an ideal but daily practice; where corruption is opposed, where citizens live peaceably as far as it depends on them, and where the Church stands at the forefront of reconciliation—drawing the nation into the peace of Christ.

In Jesus' name, Amen.

138

MONTSERRAT

Create in me a clean heart, O God; and renew a right spirit within me.
— Psalm 51:10 WEB

Sovereign Lord, King over the hills and ashes, I come as a fierce intercessor for Montserrat and proclaim that You will create a clean heart within this island people. I declare as a prophetic voice that the ruin of past eruptions will not define them—Your Spirit will renew their inner life, reordering priorities so that Christ is spoken of first and lived out daily. I take hold of Your promise to make all things new and ask that this nation's identity be forged around holiness, humility and steadfast devotion rather than mere cultural habit.

Father, breathe renewal into families and leaders whose lives were shaped by trauma, loss and displacement. Where nominal Christianity once provided comfort without transformation, now raise up worshippers who are inwardly changed and outwardly fruitful. I ask You to strengthen the small evangelical core and to awaken the historic churches to robust discipleship: Bible-saturated teaching, accountable fellowship, and practical mercy ministries for those still carrying physical and emotional scars. Let theological training, pastoral care and mentoring be prioritized so pastors will shepherd with discernment and courage.

Lord Jesus, I prophesy a new start for Montserrat in which economic and social rebuilding bears spiritual fruit. Use the realities of dependence and rebuilding to produce humility and communal care; convert hardship into an expression of God-honoring stewardship. Raise entrepreneurs and community leaders who will steward resources with wisdom and who will place Christ at the center of recovery plans. Let youth who might otherwise drift into despair discover purpose in serving the Church—trained, sent and sustained by the island's congregations.

Holy Spirit, heal the memory of disaster, knit together broken families, and root the island in a living faith that endures. I declare that Montserrat will not be remembered merely for what was lost but for the people who, by Your grace, were remade into a witnessing, prayerful community—joyful, sober, and unwavering in Christ. Let the clean heart You craft become a lamp to the nations.

In Jesus' name, Amen.

139

Morocco

> Look to me, and be saved, all the ends of the earth: for I am God, and there is no other.
> — Isaiah 45:22 WEB

Majestic Savior, the One whom nations must turn to, I stand before You on behalf of Morocco and prophesy a turning of eyes and hearts toward the only true God. I declare that the earthquake and times of calamity will become turning points where many look beyond temporal idols and see their need for the Savior. Let the memory of mourning be transformed into a season of openness: hearts softened, conversations begun, and curiosity about Jesus fostered by acts of mercy and visible love from believers.

Father, mobilize the indigenous church and faithful expatriates to be instruments of trustworthy compassion in every affected town and mountain village. Where Christians quietly served after the disaster, multiply their witness so that it becomes a recognized channel of help and hope. Strengthen the persecuted believers who meet in house fellowships; protect them from retaliation and embolden them with mutual encouragement. Grow their numbers in secret but also deepen their faith, sanity, and theological formation so they may withstand pressure and testify with clarity.

Lord Jesus, break the religious and familial pressures that oppress new believers; give courage like the early Church—mutual support, strategic discretion, and sacrificial love. Use the positive media moments of help and rescue to diminish prejudice and to open doors for Gospel conversation in hospitals, shelters, and in neighborhoods still reeling. Raise leaders who can shepherd new converts through trauma and fear, and equip networks that provide counseling, vocational support, and safe community for those who must hide for the sake of their lives.

Holy Spirit, draw many by dreams, visions, and the irresistible demonstration of love so that the Name of Jesus is trusted across Morocco. I prophesy that as people look to the One who saves, small house fellowships will multiply in humility and courage, persecution will refine rather than destroy, and new believers will stand strong—living witnesses of resurrection hope in a land thirsty for truth.

In Jesus' name, Amen.

140

MOZAMBIQUE

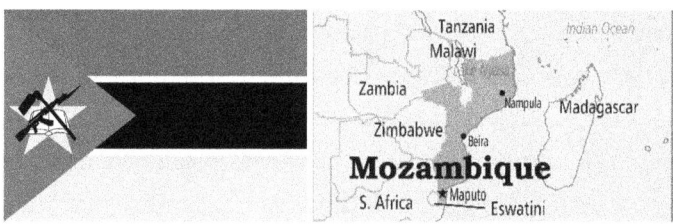

"He will deliver the needy when he cries; the poor also, and him who has no helper."
— Psalm 72:12 WEB

Lord God of justice and compassion, I bow in prayer for Mozambique and declare that You will deliver the needy, uphold the broken, and answer the cries of those without help. I prophesy an increase of gospel compassion across Maputo and the most remote provinces—churches mobilized to meet HIV/AIDS, malaria, cyclone aftermaths, and trauma with both medicine and mercy. Let the Christian community be known as the primary responder that brings healing and hope where suffering has been deepest.

Father, grant wisdom and resources to leaders and aid agencies so that public health systems expand effectively: antiretroviral programs scaled up, malaria prevention massively implemented, and mental health care for the traumatized widely available. Protect and strengthen those working in dangerous northern regions where IS-CAP and other violent actors threaten communities. Give security and supply lines to ministries that bring food, shelter, and spiritual care into hard-hit districts following climate disasters and conflict.

Lord Jesus, raise up a Church that not only evangelizes but sustains—training nurses, pastors, counselors and community organizers who work among the poor and remote. Break down denominational barriers so the Body of Christ ministers together in practical unity. Let churches establish sustainable agricultural projects, water systems, and child-care programs that stabilize families and reduce vulnerability to exploitation and radicalization. Empower local leaders with resources to rebuild after cyclones and to embed resilience into community planning.

Holy Spirit, revive the nation through tangible works of mercy allied to bold proclamation. I prophesy a Mozambique where democracy and spiritual awakening converge: where recovered villages sing of both deliverance and grace, where believers stand firm against persecution, and where the light of Christ dispels fear and brings restoration across the land. Let the needy be delivered and the nation healed.

In Jesus' name, Amen.

141

MYANMAR

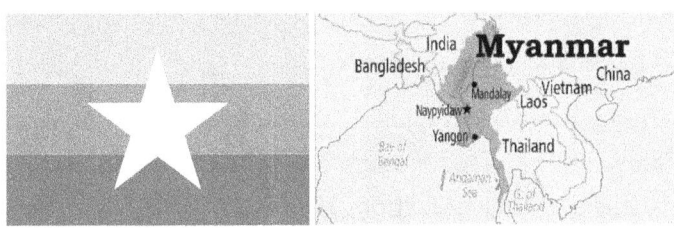

"The Spirit of the Lord is upon me, because he has anointed me to preach the gospel to the poor; he has sent me to heal the brokenhearted, to preach deliverance to the captives, and recovering of sight to the blind, to set at liberty those who are oppressed."
— Luke 4:18 WEB

Compassionate Lord and Healer of nations, I come as an intercessor for Myanmar and declare the anointing of the Spirit upon Your Church there to be poured out in power. I prophesy a movement of grace where wounds of violence, displacement, and ethnic hatred are met with the healing ministry of Christ—house churches strengthened, secret converts emboldened, and the very hearts of communities softened. Let gospel love find ways into monasteries, villages, and refugee camps so captives are set free.

Father, give supernatural unity where division has been deep. Raise peacemakers among the many ethnic groups—Kachin, Karen, Shan, Rakhine, Chin—and among Burmese majority communities who secretly seek truth. Infuse leaders with wisdom to navigate danger while pursuing reconciliation: those who can forge humanitarian corridors, facilitate trauma-informed counseling, and create sanctuaries for refugees and internally displaced people. Bring leaders to negotiate pauses in violence so aid can flow and lives can be saved.

Lord Jesus, protect and multiply the quiet work of converts from Buddhist and monastic backgrounds who are coming to Christ. Shield them from persecution, give them secret fellowship and robust discipleship, and equip them to witness gently in Buddhist cultural contexts. Empower Christian broadcasters, Scripture-based radio and clandestine discipleship materials to reach those who cannot meet openly. Bless the isolated believers with boldness and discretion, and raise up pastors trained in pastoral care for severe trauma.

Holy Spirit, move with convicting power across Myanmar: heal the brokenhearted, break chains of oppression, and open blind eyes to the Savior. I prophesy that in the midst of military oppression and ethnic strife, Your Church will be the instrument of restoration—bringing liberty, restoration, and a steady advance of the gospel that will outlast dictators and transform generations. Let peace and justice rise like a river across this beautiful land.

In Jesus' name, Amen.

Epilogue

The end of this book is not the finish line—it is a front door. If Psalm 2:8 summons you to ask, then the epilogue summons you to persevere. The nations described here will not be transformed overnight. Kingdom advance is patient and relentless, and it requires prayer that endures seasons, generations, and complex realities. What you have read and prayed through in this first book is seed; now you must water that seed with ongoing, disciplined intercession. Let this be the moment you commit to sustained prayer for the nations rather than sporadic concern.

Adopt rhythms that will carry you forward. Pray daily for one nation, or weekly through this collection; gather with others for focused monthly sessions; join or form an intercessory cohort that will hold one another accountable. Keep records—songlines of answered prayer and of lessons learned. Use Scripture as your measuring rod. Where you see corruption, declare God's justice; where you see broken families, plead for restoration; where idols still hold sway, call heaven's light to expose and displace them. Be strategic: combine knowledge (informed by resources like Operation World) with faith-filled decrees. The combination of careful information and burning intercession is lethal to principalities.

Commit also to action beyond the kneeling place. Let prayer lead to practical engagement—sending resources, supporting long-term ministry partners, advocating for justice, and training leaders. Intercession should produce involvement; asking for the nations will move your hands and feet. Teach these prayers in your church; mentor younger intercessors; model constancy. The

Church's spiritual governance over nations is exercised most powerfully when prayer and praxis are yoked together.

Finally, receive patience. Nations heal slowly, but the Lord of the nations is not slow. Your prayers are powerful and effective (James 5:16). They form a covenant-line of influence that stretches from your living room to the palaces of leaders and the huts of the most forgotten. Press on. Do not grow weary. Keep asking, keep knocking, and keep believing until the nations you pray for begin to wear the robes of the King. The inheritance is sure—the call to intercede is urgent. Rise to it. Give the nations to the Lord with persistence, passion, and prophetic precision.

In Jesus' name, Amen.

Encourage Others with Your Story

If this prayer guide has strengthened your faith, deepened your intercession, or helped you stand in the gap, would you consider leaving a short review on Amazon? Your feedback not only encourages others but also helps more believers discover this resource and join in the prayer movement. Every review—just a few sentences—makes a difference. Thank you for being part of this movement.

MORE FROM PRAYERSCRIPTS

THE HEALING COVENANT SERIES

"BRETHREN, PRAY FOR US" SERIES

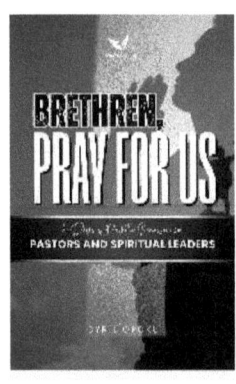 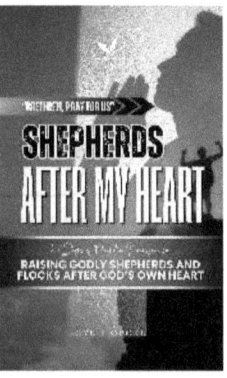 

COMMAND YOUR DESTINY SERIES

THE PRAYER OF JABEZ SERIES

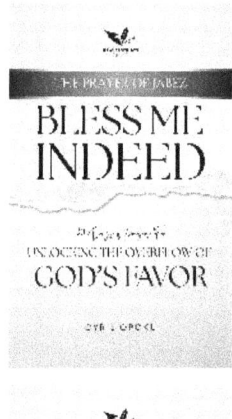
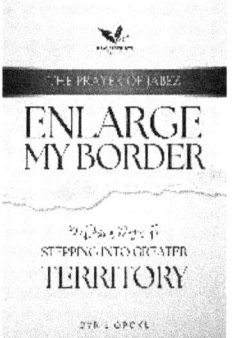
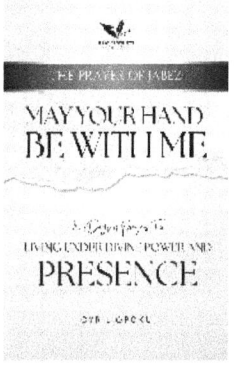

EXPOSING THE ENEMY SERIES

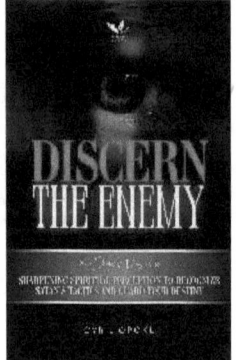

SPIRITUAL WARFARE SERIES

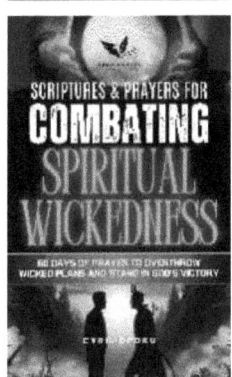 

ONE NATION UNDER GOD SERIES

ONE NATION UNDER GOD SERIES

THE BLOOD COVENANT SERIES

www.ingramcontent.com/pod-product-compliance
Lightning Source LLC
Chambersburg PA
CBHW070633160426
43194CB00009B/1451